FINDING GOD FAITHFUL

A STUDY ON
THE LIFE OF JOSEPH

KELLY MINTER

Student Ministry Publishing

Ben Trueblood
Director, Student Ministry

John Paul Basham
*Manager, Student
Ministry Publishing*

Karen Daniel
Editorial Team Leader

Mary Margaret West
Content Editor

Jennifer Siao
Production Editor

Amy Lyon
Graphic Designer

Published by LifeWay Press® • © 2019 Kelly Minter
Reprinted Oct. 2019

ISBN 978-1-5359-4547-9
Item 005812432
Dewey decimal classification: 234.2
Subject heading: JOSEPH, SON OF JACOB / FAITH / PROVIDENCE AND GOVERNMENT OF GOD

To order additional copies of this resource, write LifeWay Church Resources Customer Service; One LifeWay Plaza; Nashville, TN 37234-0113; FAX order to 615.251.5933; call toll-free 800.458.2772; email orderentry@lifeway.com *or order online at* www.lifeway.com.

Printed in the United States of America.

Student Ministry Publishing, LifeWay Church Resources, One LifeWay Plaza, Nashville, TN 37234

TABLE OF CONTENTS

MEET THE AUTHOR

KELLY MINTER is passionate about teaching the Bible, and she believes it permeates all of life. She's found personal healing and steadfast hope in the pages of Scripture. When she's not singing, writing, or speaking, you can find her picking homegrown vegetables, enjoying her six nieces and nephews, or riding a boat down the Amazon River with Justice & Mercy International. A Southern transplant, Kelly delights in neighborhood walks, watching college football, and a diner mug of good coffee with her closest friends.

Kelly's love for the Word of God led her to write in-depth Bible studies, like the one you hold in your hands. Those Bible studies include, *Ruth: Loss, Love & Legacy; Nehemiah: A Heart That Can Break; What Love Is: The Letters of 1, 2, 3 John; All Things New: A Study on 2 Corinthians; and No Other Gods: The Unrivaled Pursuit of Christ.* Kelly's music includes Hymns & Hallelujahs, which accompanies her *All Things New* Bible study.

Wherever the River Runs: How a Forgotten People Renewed My Hope in the Gospel is Kelly's first memoir about her life-changing journeys to the Amazon jungle with Justice & Mercy International (JMI). Kelly partners with JMI, an organization that cares for the vulnerable and forgotten in the Amazon and Moldova. To view more about Kelly's studies, books, music, and Cultivate events, visit www.kellyminter.com.

A NOTE FROM KELLY

Joseph's story welcomes us with open arms, summons us into the living room, and invites us to sit down awhile and listen. So many have found a dear companion in Joseph because his life displays so much of the human experience. We all "get" Joseph on some level. We can relate to him. We've probably never owned a multi-colored robe that nearly cost us our lives, or traveled as a slave by camel to a foreign land, but we understand difficult family relationships. We've experienced betrayal. We know unfair. Broken dreams have nearly sunk us. And almost every one of us has wondered at some point in our lives, *where is God?*

In *Finding God Faithful* we'll discover that as epic and important as Joseph's account is, it's actually but a tiny act in God's grand narrative of redemption, The Story. So while we study Joseph's story we will pay best attention to God's.

So what does all of this mean for us? Well, I'm glad you asked. Genesis 37-50 (Joseph's account) reveals how deeply God loves us and wants us to love others—even those most difficult to love. On a very practical level, Joseph's life will affirm that we're to run from temptation, serve when we're suffering, and serve when we're prospering. And if you've ever wondered when to protect yourself from the people who have wounded you and when to lay down your defenses, throw your arms around your foes and weep, Joseph's story doesn't give us a manual, but boy does it offer us an epic scene.

This is to say nothing of what Joseph's story teaches us about how God can take the stones thrown at us with evil intent and use them as the bedrock of His good plans for our lives. No one will ever describe the mystery quite like Joseph; "You planned evil against me; God planned it for good…" (Gen. 50:20). Which brings us to another most practical theme of Joseph's story: forgiveness. If Joseph could forgive his brothers I imagine there's no one we can't learn to forgive.

For those of you who have ever wondered if your dark nights and crushing heartbreak were sure signs that God had forgotten or abandoned you, Joseph's story confidently tells us otherwise. In a faraway land, and later in a dismal prison, what more hopeful truth could be written than "God was with Joseph"? Whether in prison or in palace, His presence changes everything. Perhaps above all, what I hope you will gather from this study is a richer understanding of God's promises, His faithfulness to His people, and the person of Jesus toward whom Joseph's entire story is aimed.

HOW TO USE

In this study you will find eight weeks of group discussion and seven weeks of personal study. The Leader Kit includes eight 15-20 minute videos of Kelly's teaching adapted specifically for girls. The first session of the study begins simply with your group getting to know one another and watching and discussing the session video. Girls will begin their Personal Study for Session 2 after your first meeting and then continue through Session 8 of Personal Study, wrapping up *Finding God Faithful* by watching the Session 8 video and completing the Viewer Guide and Group Discussion.

BIBLE STUDY BOOK

Each girl will need their own Bible study book, which includes the following elements:

Introduction
Each session's two-page introduction will set up the week ahead and give girls an idea of what they'll be studying. Session 1 does not have an introduction since it is the first meeting. The general "Note From Kelly" is what you should point girls to read as an introduction as you first begin to meet.

Viewer Guide & Group Discussion
The Viewer Guide includes the points and fill-in-the-blanks from the session's video (answers in Leader Guide). There is also space for girls to take notes as they're watching. Then use the remaining time for the Group Discussion and prayer. Feel free to adapt the Group Discussion based on your group of girls and their context.

Personal Study
There are five days of personal Bible study which can be done at your own pace and will help reinforce and prepare girls for the next session of video content that will sum up the session. It is alright if girls are unable to get to all of the personal study. Encourage them to catch up if they are behind but be understanding if it's too time-consuming for some girls to complete.

Personal Response & Personal Reflection
This content in the sidebars allows for girls to dig deeper in their application and reflection as they further consider and think through what they're studying.

LEADER GUIDE

The Leader Guide at the back of this study provides a key with answers for the Viewer Guide, in addition to leader tips, a simple guide for how to lead this Bible study, and a session-by-session guide for leaders.

LEADER KIT

You will need one Leader Kit per group. This Kit provides all the session videos you'll need, in addition to social media content that will provide additional helps. Consider using the promotional video during your student ministry gatherings as you are initially sharing about this Bible study group. The message to leaders video is also something you might want to share with other Bible study leaders if you plan to take multiple groups of girls through the study.

Social Media Content

The Share Squares will be helpful if you want to encourage girls during the week by sharing these on social media or in a group message. The promotional video is also designed to share on social media in order to get the word out to girls about the Bible study.

WordSearch

You also receive access to free commentaries and other resources in WordSearch with your purchase of the Leader Kit. These resources will help you dig deeper as you prepare to lead this Bible study.

Session One

SET APART

"You planned evil against me;
God planned it for good..."

GENESIS 50:20

SESSION ONE VIEWER GUIDE

SET APART

Fill in the blanks as you're watching the Session 1 video. If you miss any blanks, your leader should be able to help and go over these with you.

1. When God sets you apart, it's an _invitation_ to relationship with Him.

2. Being _set apart_ will always be in keeping with God's grand plan of redemption.

3. When God sets you apart for a task, He _shoulders_ the responsibility for its outcome.

4. Being set apart is initiated by God but carried out through our _obedience_.

NOTES

_____

_____

_____

_____

_____

_____

_____

_____

_____

_____

GROUP DISCUSSION

✝ Share and discuss what you want to learn and gain from this study in the coming weeks.

✝ Sometimes it's easy to get caught up in a culture that is all about us. How can we stand against the culture and seek to be a blessing to others?

✝ How does Abraham's faith to follow God into the unknown challenge encourage you?

✝ What are you waiting on the Lord for? How does Rachel's experience help you to hope in God's divine activity in your circumstances as you pray and seek Him?

✝ Why is waiting so difficult? What has God taught you in times of waiting?

✝ Have you ever found yourself in a perplexing situation in which God seems to be working contrary to your understanding of His plan? How does this turn in Joseph's life challenge you to trust God's plans and presence?

THE UNLIKELY PATH OF BLESSING

My best friend and I sat on the front stoop of my parents' old house where we talked about our future plans and dreams. I was in college at the time and she had recently graduated. I'd grown up in an intact family while both her parents had had multiple marriages. "The bus is stopping here and I'm getting off," my friend asserted. I was well acquainted with her story and knew exactly what she meant. She was choosing to be led by Christ, not defined by her family's past.

All these years later, she'd confidently tell you that by the grace of God, Jesus has defined her life apart from the generational and familial patterns that often feel as inescapable as our DNA. If I didn't believe Jesus could do this, Joseph's life that we're about to study would simply be an anomaly instead of a testimony to what God is still doing today—bringing beauty from ashes.

As we begin our study of Joseph's life we're going to see a life that, given the circumstances, shouldn't have made it out of the teenage years, much less flourished. Without giving too many of the details away, Joseph was born into a family pierced by jealousy, favoritism, and competition—even murderous rage. His family of origin had hardly set him up for success, spiritual or otherwise. On top of that, the tragic turn his life took as a young man certainly seemed irredeemable. Joseph's emergence as a humble leader who would save a nation can only be explained by the power of God to triumph over the power of our pasts.

As we begin our first week of study, I want to encourage you that your identity need not stay rooted in past failures or past sin, even a past and harmful environment you had no control over. When you surrender to Jesus, the old and frail no longer have sway over the redemptive work He promises to do in your life. If God took what was meant for evil in Joseph's life and used it for good, will He not do the same for you?

Day 1
SETTING THE STAGE
Genesis 12:1-9

My grandfather, Charles S. Minter, Jr., was an admiral in the Navy and the superintendent of the United States Naval Academy from 1964-1965. Since his death in 2008, our family has been enamored with any new bits of information about his life that turn up. My brother recently found a transcript of an interview my grandfather did in the '80s. In that transcript we found pieces of news even my father didn't know, like the fact that my grandfather's grandfather was a Presbyterian minister in Covington, Virginia.

In light of this discovery, I couldn't help but wonder if my great, great grandfather and his wife ever specifically prayed for the generations that would follow them. Did they ask God for their descendants to love Him, His Word, and His people? Of course God is always at work before any of us arrive on the scene, but it's been interesting to consider the ways He might have been working before me in my ancestors.

Joseph's story will be far more meaningful to us once we understand how God moved in the people before Joseph.

Similarly, I believe understanding Joseph's story will be far more meaningful to us once we understand how God moved in the people before Joseph. We'll trace some of those happenings so we can best appreciate what God was doing in the lives of Joseph, his brothers, all of Israel, and eventually you and me. But not all today—sorry, if I just stressed you out, because I just got a little overwhelmed myself.

LET'S BEGIN OUR STUDY BY READING GENESIS 11:31–12:9.

According to Genesis 11:31, where was Abraham living when God called him to leave? (Note: God would later change Abram's name to Abraham in Gen. 17:5, so I'll refer to him as the latter.)

Pulling your answer only from Genesis 12:1, to what land did God call Abraham to go?

RESPOND: Try to imagine being in Abraham's position. How would God's vague instructions about your future destination been difficult for you? For example: when it comes to college, boyfriends, jobs, and so on.

According to Genesis 12:3, who specifically would be blessed through Abraham as a result of his obedience to God's leading?

God's covenant with Abraham is the bedrock of our study, so we're going to look at three promises God made to Abraham:
1. Land: God promised Abraham and his people the promised land of Canaan.
2. Descendants: God promised to multiply Abraham's descendants, making nations come from him.
3. Blessing: God promised to bless Abraham and to bless all the peoples of the world through Abraham.

By majestic grace, God pulled Abraham from his father's family, a family that served other gods (Josh. 24:2), and told Abraham He would bless Abraham, multiply his family, and make him into a blessing for the whole world. And there began the beginning of Israel's history.

Note: Joseph was born only two generations after God's covenant with Abraham. This is important to remember.

READ GALATIANS 3:7-9.

In verse 8, the apostle Paul quoted from Genesis 12:3. As part of God's promise to Abraham that all nations would be blessed, who has God justified?

What is required to be blessed through Abraham? Paul uses the word four times in these verses. (Circle the best answer below.)

| *Belief* | *Righteousness* | *Faith* | *Passion* |

We're left with the question: *Faith in what?* The prevailing thought of our day is to have faith in yourself and believe that you're enough. I know myself too well to feel good about this premise. We see another widely accepted option in our current culture: put your faith in how many likes you get on Instagram, being on trend with your clothes and accessories, doing good things for others, and so on. The apostle Paul helps us narrow this down.

CONTINUE READING GALATIANS 3; LET'S MOVE TO VERSES 13-14.

I will bless those who bless you, I will curse anyone who treats you with contempt, and all the peoples on earth will be blessed through you.

GENESIS 12:3

*Who redeemed us and therefore is the only one worthy of our faith?
What did Jesus redeem us from?*

What did we receive as part of God's promise to Abraham?

The connections that Paul makes between God's covenant with Abraham and Jesus' redemption of the Gentiles will continue to crystalize throughout our study. You and I are part of the fulfillment of the promise God made to Abraham all those thousands of years ago in the desert of Haran, a promise He later affirmed in the land of Canaan.

READ GENESIS 17:15-19.

*Ishmael was the son of Abraham and Hagar, Sarah's maidservant;
Isaac was the son of Abraham and Sarah. Through which son would
God's covenant with Abraham continue? (Circle the correct answer.)*

    Ishmael   *Isaac*

READ GENESIS 25:19-20,22-26 & 28:1-4.

*With which of Rebekah and Isaac's sons did God confirm His
covenant? (Circle the correct answer.)*

    Jacob   *Esau*

READ GENESIS 29:21-28.

What two women did Jacob marry?

*So far we've learned that God made a covenant with Abraham.
God then confirmed that covenant through Abraham and Sarah's
son,_____. He continued to confirm it through Isaac and
Rebekah's son, _____.*

We're now circling in on the central figure of our story: Joseph.

READ GENESIS 30:22-24.

*Begin filling out the family tree on page 18. Joseph's father was
_____and his mother was _____.*

JACOB'S FAMILY TREE

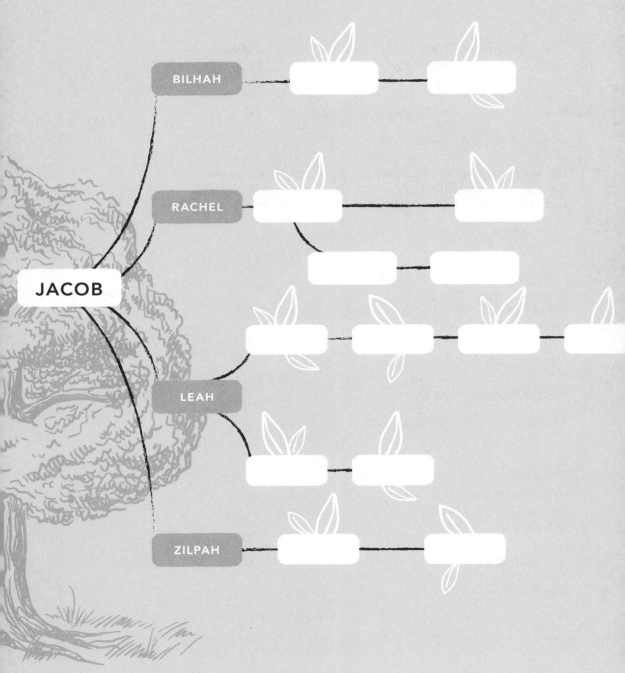

JACOB

BILHAH

RACHEL

LEAH

ZILPAH

You've pieced a lot of genealogical information together today. Well done! Now I want to briefly return to where we began—Genesis 12:1. This verse perfectly sums up our faith journey, doesn't it? At some point in our walks with Christ we have to let go of what we think we know is best and take hold of what He says is best. God doesn't often give us a clear picture of where we're going, only a clear picture of Himself so we can follow Him there.

While Abraham's faith is inspiring, I'm grateful that God's covenant plan didn't rest on a human's faith but on God's own promises, which are secured in His character.

Day 2
BORN INTO DRAMA
Genesis 29:16–30:24

It's really easy to see that your family of origin (the family you were raised in) has a direct effect on your development and who you become. Thankfully, our families of origin don't have to dictate the trajectories of our lives—especially with the indwelling of the Holy Spirit who has the power to renew us and break through generational patterns of unhealthy and destructive behavior (2 Cor. 10:3-4). Exploring the family Joseph was born into will give us a clearer picture of who he was and the struggles he faced. Today is going to be fun, if for no other reason than we'll be dealing with someone else's drama instead of our own.

READ GENESIS 29:16-30. YOU COVERED SOME OF THIS PASSAGE YESTERDAY, BUT READ IT AGAIN IN VIEW OF LEAH'S PLIGHT.

RESPOND: In what ways did Laban set up Leah for heartache and rejection? How might this have affected her overall well-being as a wife and mother?

READ GENESIS 29:31–30:24.

What did Rachel have that Leah desperately wanted? What did Leah have that Rachel desperately wanted?

God's remembering us will never be separated from His divine activity and His perfect timing in our lives.

What did Leah hope having children would do for her relationship with Jacob? List every hope. (See Gen. 29:32,34; 30:20.)

Even though Jacob chose Rachel as the love of his life, describe her overall state in Genesis 30:1.

Then God remembered Rachel.

GENESIS 30:22a

How did Rachel try to "fix" her problem of not being able to bear children?

Remember, we began our study by looking at God's covenant with Abraham—to bless his family and bring a great nation from him. So far it isn't looking as promising as I would have hoped.

Go to page 18, and fill in the rest of the family tree with the names you read about today. This will help you continue to piece together God's covenant through Abraham's family, particularly the role Joseph will play. (For a quick list of names, go to Gen. 35:23-26.)

LOOK BACK AT GENESIS 30:22-24.

What did Rachel say had been taken away from her when Joseph was born?

The Hebrew word used here for disgrace is *herpâ*, and it means a "state of dishonor and low status."[1] In ancient Hebrew culture a woman's worth was bound up in her family. Her legacy was based on her ability to bear children, especially sons, who would carry on the family name.

Remembered is another important word in verse 22, "Then God *remembered* Rachel" (*emphasis mine*). First, "when the Lord 'remembers' in Genesis and Exodus, this activity is often tied to God's covenant with Israel."[2] By using the word, *remembered*, the narrator is signaling to us that God's upcoming work in Rachel's life is significant to His covenant with Abraham and the future nation of Israel. Rachel is part of a grander story.

The word *remember* in the Old Testament also indicates God's action. This might be confusing for us because our modern usage of *remember* gives the impression that for all these years God had forgotten Rachel. Fortunately, this is not what the word means here at all.

God's remembering us will never be separated from His divine activity and His perfect timing in our lives. Though Rachel had prayed for many years, seemingly to no avail, God heard her prayers and had a far greater plan than she could have imagined.

While it's good to wait on God for the things we long for, the way we wait on Him is even more important. In your waiting, tell the Lord you trust His timing and believe in His power to achieve your heart's desire. Surrender your agenda to Him. And where your faith lacks, pray these words from Mark 9:24, "I do believe; help my unbelief!"

Thankfully, the God who transforms our hearts hasn't changed.

God acted at just the right time. Abraham's descendants were a bit of a mess, yes, but grace showed up anyway in the arms of a broken woman named Rachel, in the form of a baby boy named Joseph, by the power of Yahweh, the God of Israel.

Day 3

FAVORITISM AND JEALOUSY

Genesis 37:1-11

Today we step onto the soil where Joseph grew up. We find him as a seventeen-year-old tending sheep with his brothers in the midst of complex family dynamics, many of which stemmed from the favoritism of his father and the jealousy of his brothers. If you'd hoped we could ease into Joseph's story with a latte and a "once upon a time" opening line, the author of Genesis gives us no such luxury. Instead he takes the more direct approach of immediately plunging us into the middle of a dysfunctional family. Thankfully, the God who transforms our hearts hasn't changed. And with that hopeful reminder, we'll begin our story.

READ GENESIS 37:1-11.

Write down anything that stands out to you from these verses and explain why it stands out.

Compare Genesis 37:3 with Genesis 25:27-28 and 29:30. What problematic similarities do you see in these passages?

Look back at Genesis 33:1-3. What generational seed planted by Isaac and Rebekah showed up in Jacob's marriage and parenting?

As we address the deeper issues of favoritism and jealousy that fractured Jacob's family, my prayer is for God to bring healing to our relationships that may be broken in similar ways and for similar reasons.

Doing something for someone based on what I'll receive in return can be an indicator of unhealthy favoritism, as is doing something for someone out of fear of losing them. Perhaps the simplest way of putting it is this: While love and friendship are based on selflessness, favoritism is typically based on selfishness.

TURN TO THE NEW TESTAMENT AND READ JAMES 2:1-9.

Why did the person in this example show favoritism to the one and not the other?

Why does James specifically say we shouldn't show favoritism?

And the fruit of righteousness is sown in peace by those who cultivate peace.

JAMES 3:18

When we show favoritism to someone, we don't do so in isolation; others in our lives are affected. In the James passage, because the rich person was favored the poor person was obviously shamed. Likewise, in Genesis, Joseph's brothers were hurt by Jacob's favoritism of him.

List the strong words of animosity used to describe the brothers' feelings toward Joseph. (See Gen. 37:4-5,8,11.)

I've often wondered why Joseph shared his dreams with his brothers. Did he do it out of excitement or spite? Did he hope they might start showing him respect? I'm reminded here of the importance of pure motives and wise timing when we talk about the good and exciting things in our lives—even the things *God* is doing. While we can't make others be jealous of us, we don't want to unwisely foster it.

RESPOND: In our age of social media, how can you be more thoughtful about what you choose to share and not share based on today's passages?

Because of Joseph's dreams and Jacob's partiality toward Joseph, the brothers allowed jealousy to overtake their hearts and determine their decisions.

TURN BACK TO JAMES AND READ VERSES 3:13-18.

RESPOND: Is there anyone you're jealous of right now? If so, write down the reason behind your jealousy.

PERSONAL RESPONSE

If favoritism has affected your family, friendships, or school relationships, describe its effects below.

James describes what happens when selfish ambitions rule our lives and relationships. But he also paints an inspiring picture of a person whose life is characterized by wisdom that's pure, gentle, and full of mercy and peace. When I'm given to jealousy I look nothing like this wise, gentle, and peaceful person.

I don't know what jealousy looks like on you, but it looks terrible on me—worse than the time I cut my own bangs in junior high and thought wearing a pink bandanna would help. Truth.

In my place of longing God has invited me to trust Him and His goodness. And when I'm secure in His provision, I can be happy for those around me. My character becomes marked by peace and kindness, not the worldly wisdom of envying others and tirelessly grasping for what I want.

RESPOND: Think about someone you are jealous of and confess your jealousy to the Lord. Confess whatever it is this person has that you desperately want. Ask God to meet that need in you however He desires. He is good and delights to give good gifts to you (Matt. 7:9-11).

The true beauty of Joseph's story is that in the midst of favoritism, jealousy, and anger, God is working out His purposes. His covenant promises will prevail despite the sin and brokenness of the people to whom the promises were made. God is faithful. We know that He is altogether good and doesn't show favoritism (Acts 10:34; Rom. 2:11). I wish Jacob and the brothers could have known that Joseph's dreams would prove to be good news for them, that they were part of God's story, as well. By the end of our study together, I hope you, too, will be convinced of this.

Day 4

WHEN WE DON'T UNDERSTAND

Genesis 37:12-28

As you read today's passage, be on the lookout for God's providential hand throughout the narrative. It's easy for us to think of God as being "way up there" in the heavens on His end of the universe while we plod along in our daily lives with little intervention from Him. But here in Genesis, long before the incarnation of Jesus, we see God at work on earth. We see Him moving in specific locations on the map, guiding people, orchestrating events, and working out His covenant promises.

So now, come on, let's kill him and throw him into one of the pits. We can say that a vicious animal ate him. Then we'll see what becomes of his dreams!

GENESIS 37:20

MEDITERRANEAN SEA

DOTHAN

SHECHEM

HEBRON VALLEY

EGYPT

JOSEPH'S JOURNEY

From memory, God's covenant with Abraham consisted of what three promises? (See Day 1 of this week if you need help.)

1.

2.

3.

Little did Jacob know that when he sent his beloved son Joseph on a journey to find his brothers, Jacob wouldn't see Joseph again for over twenty years. And Jacob would never again see Joseph in the land of Canaan.

Joseph searched for his brothers by traveling north from the Hebron Valley to a place called Shechem. According to Genesis 12:6-7, what significant event took place in Shechem?

Is there someone at school who is being bullied or pushed to the side who the Lord is asking you to protect, defend, or stand up for? Write that person's name below and what you feel prompted to do on his or her behalf.

Who do you think is the unnamed man in Genesis 37:15-17?

Jewish tradition views this man as an angel.[3] I don't think we can know for sure who he is, but in the words of K.A. Matthews,

Whether the "man" is an angel or a human, the unseen hand of the Lord is apparent here.[4]

RESPOND: At just the sight of Joseph in the distance the brothers began plotting to kill him. Genesis 37:19 gives us further insight into the reason behind their hatred. What was their reason, and why do you think it bothered them to the point of wanting to murder their brother?

We'll come back to the last sentence of Genesis 37:20 at the very end of our study. But, I want you to hang on to it throughout our time together, so finish the passage below.

"So, now, come on, let's kill him and throw him into one of the pits. We can say that a vicious animal ate him. Then we'll see _____ _____ !" (CSB).

Out of the darkness flickered a bit of brotherly care and protection as Reuben pleaded with his brothers, urging them to throw Joseph into a dry cistern instead of killing him. We're told that Reuben suggested this plan so he could later rescue Joseph and return him to their father. Whatever Reuben's motives, it's a reminder to us that speaking up for

what's right can have enormous impact. Maybe even save a person's life. Or thousands of lives.

The brothers' murderous plotting may be an extreme case, but the principle remains. It's easy to go along with the current of the crowd instead of risking something for the sake of an individual.

> *According to Genesis 37:26, what was Judah's motive for deciding not to kill Joseph?*

Joseph was sold for twenty pieces of silver, the going rate for a healthy young man in the early second millennium. People from the land of Canaan are commonly found in Egyptian records as slaves in various roles.[5] You would think that approximately four thousand years after this horrific scene human trafficking would be wiped clean from our world. Tragically, it is still happening all over the globe, even in our own backyards. (See note below.)

After reading today's portion of Joseph's story it seems as though God has lost control. It appeared Joseph was being kicked around the landscape like a rubber ball on an elementary playground. His father sent him to Shechem, a mysterious man redirected him to Dothan, then his brothers after deciding not to kill him, secured him a one-way ticket to Egypt by way of Ishmaelite traders.

We won't solve the problem of why a good God allows suffering, nor will we fully understand God's sovereignty at the end of our eight weeks together. But my prayer is that we'll better understand both suffering and sovereignty from the perspective of God's Word, so that we'll see His hand more clearly and trust His heart more deeply. Our God is good.

RESPOND: What stood out to you the most in today's personal study and why?

Joseph's brothers may have been able to destroy his coat of many colors, but they would never be able to destroy the dreams God had given him. Remember that, girls.

Note: *If the Lord is stirring in your heart to help fight against human trafficking, there are many organizations doing this important work. I trust and work alongside is Justice & Mercy International an organization that stops trafficking in the developing Eastern European country of Moldova before it happens. To find out more, visit justiceandmercy.org.*

Day 5
GOD WAS WITH JOSEPH

Genesis 37:29-36; 39:1-6

We can get through just about any pain or suffering if we know the Lord is in it with us. But when we feel forsaken or abandoned, our pain becomes unbearable. In a most trying circumstance, the psalmist expressed what the Lord's presence meant to him with the imagery, "Even when I go through the darkest valley, I fear no danger, for *you are with me*; your rod and your staff—they comfort me" (Ps. 23:4, *emphasis mine*). In Genesis 39, we'll see the reoccurring phrase, "The LORD was with Joseph." Joseph's entire story rests on these five words. We will see how God will be everything for Joseph.

READ GENESIS 37:29-36.

In what ways did the brothers deceive Jacob without flatly lying to him, and why is this especially troubling?

We're not sure where Reuben, the firstborn, went in between the brothers throwing Joseph into the pit and Joseph being sold to the Midianites. Reuben's absence, however, made way for Judah, the fourth born, to execute his own plan without interference. These may seem like subtle details but Judah's influence over his brothers and his rising position will prove significant later.

Look back at verses 33-35. What was so puzzling about Jacob's sons trying to comfort him?

I'm trying to picture the scene: the brothers circled around their dad speaking comforting words to him, embracing him with loud cries, knowing all the while that his son wasn't dead, rather that he'd been sold at their very hands. Based on the brothers' fabricated evidence, Jacob drew his own conclusion that Joseph had been devoured by an animal.

While we're quick to condemn the brothers for their deceit, how many times have we tried to comfort someone we've hurt without first admitting the pain we've inflicted upon them? How many times have we tried to make amends without first giving an honest and heartfelt confession?

Into what nation was Joseph sold and to what person?

We began our study with God's call on Abraham's life and the covenant God made with him. Based on the land that God promised to give Abraham and his descendants in Genesis 12:4-7, why would arriving in Egypt have been particularly difficult for Joseph to process?

NOW LOOK UP GENESIS 15:13-14.

How might Joseph's forced trip to Egypt be linked to this prophecy God gave Abraham?

PERSONAL RESPONSE

We're not given much detail, but how do you think Potiphar was able to clearly tell that God was with Joseph?

Many years before Joseph's descent into Egypt God foretold that the Israelites would be enslaved in a foreign land. We don't know if Joseph was aware of this revelation, but it shows us that God's hand was on Joseph's steps even though his journey must have felt fully to the contrary. (Note: I'm not suggesting that the evil plan of the brothers or being sold into slavery were somehow good things because God's plan was being worked out. We'll later hear Joseph refer to his brothers' actions as plainly evil.) The interplay between God's sovereignty and human evil is a mystery for the ages, but what I'm hoping you'll see is that what must have felt entirely out of God's will for Joseph (arriving in Egypt) was actually part of God's plan (Israel enslaved in Egypt for four hundred years).

Whether Joseph knew it or not, what information do we find at the top of Genesis 39:2 that will prove to change everything?

Whenever you see the name LORD in small caps in your Bible, it means *Yahweh*, the personal name God Himself would give to the Israelites through Moses (Ex. 3:13-15). It's a name that would remind Israel of the covenant God made with them and of His self-existence, among other realities. The fact that the God of Israel was with Joseph in the far away and pagan land of Egypt is so profound and comforting. We simply can't imagine God's reach.

What two things about the LORD does Potiphar recognize, according to Genesis 39:3?

According to the passages below, what will cause others to see Jesus in our lives? Write your response next to each reference.

❑ *John 13:34-35*

❑ *I Thessalonians 1:4-7*

Looking closely at Genesis 39:5, what was on Potiphar's household and all that he owned? The Lord's _____. Circle the correct answer below:

Revelation   Blessing   Kindness   Judgment

In our western culture, we tend to think of God's blessing and our suffering as mutually exclusive. We think of blessing as all the good things happening in the middle of all the good times. But in Joseph's story we discover something that challenges our mindset, even as believers: certain blessings can only come in the midst of our suffering. In Egypt, Joseph was rising in power and position. Still, all these blessings fell upon Joseph in a land far away from his family and in a culture that didn't worship his God. The blessings were abounding in the midst of his suffering.

RESPOND: Are you refusing God's blessings in the midst of your trial? Surrender your pain to the Lord and tell Him you're willing to receive His blessings even if they look different than what you're hoping for.

I give you a new command: Love one another. Just as I have loved you, you are also to love one another. By this everyone will know that you are my disciples, if you love one another.

JOHN 13:34-35

Next week we'll begin an exciting five days of study in the next chapter of Joseph's life. Take some time to process what you've learned and experienced this week. Keep asking the Holy Spirit to teach His Word to you, and thank Him for His presence on the journey.

SESSION TWO VIEWER GUIDE

THE UNLIKELY PATH OF BLESSING

Fill in the blanks as you're watching the Session 2 video. If you miss any blanks, your leader should be able to help and go over these with you.

1. God can create a path of blessing even out of the most _____ circumstances.

2. Certain _____ can only come in the midst of suffering.

3. God's blessing on our lives will _____ _____ those we think He is least likely to bless.

4. The God of promise is better than the _____ _____ _____.

NOTES

_____

_____

_____

_____

_____

_____

_____

_____

✢ What part of Kelly's teaching really resonated with you? Why?

✢ Discuss the many ways favoritism damaged Jacob's family. How is it damaging to our relationships?

✢ How have you seen God create a path of blessing out of difficult circumstances? Explain.

✢ Have you ever felt like God has lost control of your story? Explain.

✢ How has God evidenced His presence in your life in your most difficult moments?

✢ Turn to 2 Corinthians 1:3-5. What is one of the purposes of our suffering (v. 4)?

✢ Have you ever been unhappy with the people God has assigned you to? Have you ever thought: I could do a great job for the Lord if He had just given me different family members, classmates, or a better church?

✢ God often uses suffering to make us fit for the dreams He has for us. The question is, are you willing to be obedient to the Lord during these seasons of testing?

FAITHFUL IN BROKENNESS

The street I live on is peppered with old-timers and relative newcomers like myself. Its rich diversity runs end to end. We're a front-porch-dwelling collection of friends and acquaintances who often stop to chat, especially during the spring and summer months when everyone's outdoors tending grills, pulling weeds, or pushing strollers up and down the hill. Miss Johnson was the queen of conversation, the unofficial mayor of our neighborhood, and the retired head of the beautifying committee. Rarely could you pass her house without receiving some sort of a resounding greeting or inquiry from her. "Well now, Kelly," she'd say to me, "How are them tomatoes doing this year?" Translation: Bring me some right now, young lady. When Miss Johnson suddenly had a stroke, it was a neighborhood affair. I encountered the trove of long-standing relationships that is our street—relationships she'd helped us build. Miss Johnson is now housebound, and unable to see, walk, or feed herself. We all miss her personality so. But none as much as her best friend Miss Meyers.

The other day I visited with Miss Meyers, who lives just a few doors down from me. She told me that she'd just been by to visit Miss Johnson. "Oh darling, it's so hard to go in there," she lamented. "Hard to see my best friend that way. It takes every single thing I got just to stay in there 30 minutes, having to watch her suffer." She paused for a moment. "But you know what Jesus says, now don't-cha? 'When I was sick, you visited Me…. Whatever you do unto the least of these, you do unto *Me*.'" Miss Meyers' eighty-something year old finger pointed my direction as she spoke. Somehow I didn't feel scolded in the least. I felt reminded, reminded of the important message God tells us from the beginning of Scripture to the end: love one another with everything you've got, because this is how Jesus loves you.

Sometimes we mistakenly think that the God of the Old Testament suddenly got nice when the Jesus of the New Testament showed up. But God has *always* cared about the poor, outcast, outsider, and sick. He's *always* commanded His people to sacrificially love others. I'm anxious for you to follow Joseph's story this week because even Joseph's own suffering won't give him a pass from loving the people around him. In fact, we'll find him serving others in the midst of his pain, and this ministry will prove to be some of his most significant.

I'm glad I strolled by Miss Meyers' this week. Glad she wasn't afraid to remind me about Jesus' command to love others, in particular our sweet friend Miss Johnson. And glad that this week Joseph won't let us forget that God has been in the business of love all along.

<h1>Day 1</h1>

<h1>TEMPTATION</h1>

<h3>Genesis 39:6-18</h3>

It seems we are never more susceptible to a major act of sin than when we're suffering. Welcome to Session 3 of our study on the life of Joseph. Today we'll be looking at the particularly human experience of temptation. While several places in Scripture tell us how to deal with temptation, I'm grateful Joseph shows us how.

TAKE YOUR TIME WITH THE TEXT TODAY. READ GENESIS 39:1-18. (YOU READ VERSES 1-6 AT THE CLOSE OF LAST WEEK, BUT REFRESH YOUR MEMORY BY BEGINNING WITH VERSE 1 TODAY.)

Verse 6 gives us some important details: What does this verse tell us about Joseph's authority and power in Potiphar's house? What does it tell us about Joseph's appearance?

RESPOND: How can the combination of these two characteristics sometimes be problematic, especially if someone is not yielded to the Lord?

PERSONAL RESPONSE

How have you played games with temptation instead of simply fleeing it? If you're in a tempting situation now, detail your plan of escape. According to Paul, the Lord has already provided you with one.

What do we find out in verse 10 about how long Potiphar's wife seduced Joseph?

The length of temptation is often part of what makes temptation so tempting. It's hard to resist something desirable over and over again. It's hard to say no for a long season.

READ GENESIS 2:15-17.

We're often tempted by the one thing we're not supposed to have. In Adam and Eve's case, God withheld nothing from them except the tree of the knowledge of good and evil. In Joseph's case, Potiphar withheld nothing from Joseph except Potiphar's wife.

RESPOND: Eve saw God as selfishly withholding from her. Why do you think Joseph didn't view Potiphar's wife as something God was withholding from him?

Returning to today's text, list all the reasons Joseph gave for not sleeping with Potiphar's wife (vv. 8-9). How do you think each of them strengthened him to stand firm?

Have you ever given into temptation because you thought you deserved the person or pleasure it was offering? Have you succumbed because God "hasn't shown up" for you in a while? Has your situation become so lonely and your rejection so painful that you think, *surely my actions are justified*? I've been there, and I understand that struggle from a deeply empathetic place in my heart. That's why I'm thankful God preserved the account of Joseph resisting temptation in a lonely and painful time in his life for us to read. Joseph's reasons for resisting temptation during a lonely and painful time can help protect us from temptation's harm.

Sin's affect on others is often something we don't think about until we see it all unfold. Joseph believed that sleeping with Potiphar's wife would affect more than just himself. How have you seen someone's sin impact people around them?

When faced with temptation, considering the consequences and impact sin will have on our relationship with God, with others, and ourselves will keep us from giving in.

LOOK BACK AT GENESIS 39:10-12.

How did Joseph escape this final temptation from Potiphar's wife?

READ 1 CORINTHIANS 10:13.

How does this verse relate to Joseph's actions?

What four truths does Paul reveal to us in 1 Corinthians 10:13?

1. The temptations that come upon us are _____.

2. God is _____.

3. God will not allow us to be tempted beyond what _____.

4. With temptation, God will also provide _____.

It's just like the enemy to tell you that you're the only one who deals with a particular temptation. This blatant lie will cause you to feel powerless against temptation, as if giving in is your only option. On the other hand, we're empowered when we humble ourselves enough to recognize that every temptation we deal with is something others have experienced and are experiencing. Your temptation is not unique. God always provides a way out. God gave Joseph two legs to run on and a door of escape to run through. That was all he needed.

Day 2
GOD'S KINDNESS
Genesis 39:19-23; 40:1-4

Today we're entering a new stretch in Joseph's story. After faithfully withstanding the temptations of Potiphar's wife, Joseph's world is about to change yet again.

BEGIN YOUR READING IN GENESIS 39:13-20 EVEN THOUGH YOU READ SOME OF THIS YESTERDAY.

Just when you thought Joseph's circumstances couldn't bring him any lower, he was thrown in prison. When something goes wrong, I have to fend off thoughts like, *How come this always happens to me?* Or, *This is so my life!* My prayer for us is to break out of the woe-is-me cycle as we look not only at Joseph's faithfulness in suffering, but God's kindness to Joseph in the midst of it. We're going to take a sword to self-wallowing today and find joy where we are because God is with us.

CONTINUE READING, IN GENESIS 39:21-23.

According to verse 21, who went to prison with Joseph?

Detail some of the ways that God showed kindness to Joseph (vv. 21-23).

Over the years, I've realized there's a difference between God's kindness and His deliverance. In our trying circumstances, all we want is for God to deliver us. But sometimes He chooses to keep us where we are so we can learn the blessing of His presence and His specific kindness to us in our trials. When that day of deliverance finally does come, we'll be ready for what's on the other side.

What phrase is mentioned twice in Genesis 39:21-23, and why do you think the author chose to emphasize it?

RESPOND: What evidences of God's presence and kindness can you identify in your current trial(s)? Pause and thank Him for these—a spirit of gratitude will combat the natural tendency to turn inward and become self-focused.

CONTINUE READING, IN GENESIS 40:1-4.

If we look at this part of the story through a human lens, we will only see an abandoned Joseph whose obedience and faithfulness had gotten him nowhere but in a prison. Sometimes the Lord has to take us lower to orchestrate His bringing us to future, breathtaking heights. Will you trust Him where He has you?

Oh, and I should mention that trusting God doesn't mean laying back, doing nothing, eating chips, and binge watching television while you wait for God to get you outta here! God never tables His call on your life. There's always work to be done.

What specific role did Joseph have while in prison (v. 4)? Which two high-ranking Egyptian officials had Joseph been assigned to?

God never tables His call on your life. There's always work to be done.

To be the chief cupbearer or baker in Pharaoh's court was to hold a prominent position of influence. (Later in Scripture we find that Nehemiah was cupbearer to King Artaxerxes.) The cupbearer opened and tasted the wine, ensuring its quality before serving it to Pharaoh.[1] The baker was in charge of a vast variety of baked goods in the royal palace.[2] The captain of the guards, possibly Potiphar (Gen. 39:1), assigned Joseph to these men (your Bible translation may say *appointed* or *put in charge of*). As a young Hebrew slave, Joseph was a servant to high-ranking Egyptian officials.

Joseph's faithfulness in the assignments God gave him challenges me because he didn't put conditions on God. He humbly served two people from a foreign country who served other gods and would have naturally despised his Hebrew heritage.

RESPOND: Is there someone that God has called you to love and serve whom you simply don't want to? Write about the relationship below.

The psalmist gives us additional information about what God was accomplishing in Joseph's life during his days in the prison.

He called down famine against the land and destroyed the entire food supply. He had sent a man ahead of them— Joseph, who was sold as a slave. They hurt his feet with shackles; his neck was put in an iron collar. Until the time his prediction came true, the word of the LORD tested him.

Psalm 105:16-19

The word *tested* here means, *to refine, purify, remove the impurities.* It also means "to purge gold or silver by fire, and to separate from dross."[3]

God doesn't test us so He can find out what's in our hearts—He already knows that. And He doesn't test us to see whether we're going to pass or fail as if He were a calculus teacher. He tests us to grow us, strengthen us, refine us. The imagery of gold being purified by fire is a certain process of purification. The testing doesn't depend on what's passing through the fire, but the sureness of the fire to remove the impurities. Sometimes we need to receive the purifying and sanctifying words of God until that deliverance comes.

What had Joseph's dreams predicted about his future? (Look back at Gen. 37:5-10 to refresh your memory.)

PERSONAL RESPONSE

What insight does the psalmist give us about this particular time in Joseph's life? What was God accomplishing in Joseph?

God was not the source of the lies and deceptions from Potiphar's wife. He did not create Potiphar's fury, the fury that led Potiphar to throw Joseph in prison unjustly. However, I do believe that God used this evil to make Joseph ready for the grand tasks ahead.

RESPOND: How do you see Joseph's time in the prison as a refiner's fire preparing him for what was coming, bringing him forth as gold?

Day 3

FORGOTTEN BUT NOT FORSAKEN

Genesis 40:5-23

Sometimes I'm exceptionally keen to God's work in my life and surroundings. In those times almost every encounter seems divinely inspired, Scripture is leaping off the page, and every worship song at church is my favorite. Then there are all the other times—where God is working because He says He is, but I don't necessarily see it or sense it.

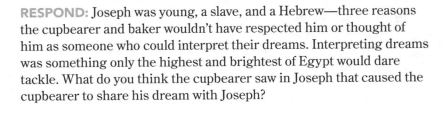

READ GENESIS 40:5-19.

RESPOND: Joseph was young, a slave, and a Hebrew—three reasons the cupbearer and baker wouldn't have respected him or thought of him as someone who could interpret their dreams. Interpreting dreams was something only the highest and brightest of Egypt would dare tackle. What do you think the cupbearer saw in Joseph that caused the cupbearer to share his dream with Joseph?

PERSONAL RESPONSE

If you're willing to serve God faithfully right where you are, write out a prayer below dedicating yourself and your circumstances to Him. Claim His presence with you and favor upon you.

We know from other verses that Joseph spent at least two years in the prison and that God was at work every single day Joseph was there. What we don't think as much about are the ways God was simultaneously working on the outside where the rest of the world was going about their lives—the part Joseph couldn't see.

Who did the cupbearer and baker work for before being thrown in prison? (See Gen. 40:2 to refresh your memory.) How might this detail be a strategic part of God's plan for Joseph?

Look back at verse 5, and fill in the blank.
Each dream had its own _____.

According to verse 8, why were the cupbearer and baker distressed?

In verse 6, the word *distraught* (or dejected, troubled) that's used to describe the state of the two officials is a strong Hebrew word. It can mean *a raging storm, anger, or a state of discouragement that is so strong one's appearance is affected.*[4] How often are we distraught because we can't make sense of something?

When Joseph noticed that the two officials were distraught, how did he respond (v. 7)? (Circle the best answer below.)

Reprimanded them   *Encouraged them*

Asked them a question   *Fed them*

Taking notice of people, asking them how they're doing, and being a good listener are some of the most powerful ministry acts we can offer. In our busy society we either don't make time to ask others how they're doing, or we simply avoid asking them because we're afraid they might actually tell us! And then what would be required of us? *Better not to ask*, we think.

I have dreams all the time that I have no explanation for. By the time I get to my coffee in the mornings, I've usually forgotten about them. In Joseph's time, however, dreams were considered one of the primary ways a person received divine revelation. In Pharaoh's court, professional magicians and counselors were tapped to reveal the meaning of these dreams. The chief cupbearer and baker were distraught not because they'd had dreams but because they were cut off from the men they believed could interpret their dreams. Joseph, the Hebrew slave boy, was their only hope.

As you're going through this Bible study as a younger woman, take courage from Joseph's example and also from Paul's words to his young son in the faith, Timothy, in 1 Timothy 4:12.

RESPOND: If God is the only One who can interpret dreams, why do you think Joseph told the men to share their dreams with him instead of with God (v. 8)?

Don't let anyone despise your youth, but set an example for the believers in speech, in conduct, in love, in faith, and in purity.

1 TIMOTHY 4:12

While it seems natural for Joseph to credit God as the interpreter of dreams, the Egyptians didn't worship the one true God. They depended on their own wise men and scientists for such divine interpretations. Here Joseph is introducing the God of his Hebrew fathers to pagan Egyptians. Anyone see an early glimpse of the gospel here?

> *Describe the meanings of each person's respective dreams, according to Joseph:*
>
> ❏ *Chief Cupbearer*
>
> ❏ *Chief Baker*

Verses 14-15 offer us the first glimpse into Joseph's heart and thoughts. Up until this point, we haven't received any insight into Joseph's feelings about the injustice he's experienced. Stating his innocence he says, "I have done nothing that they should put me in the dungeon" (Gen. 40:15b). The word used for *dungeon* is the same word used in 37:20 to describe the cistern Joseph's brothers threw him into. In other words, Joseph is saying, *I've gone from dungeon to dungeon!*[5]

RESPOND: How do these verses help you better understand what Joseph was going through internally?

CONTINUE READING, IN GENESIS 40:20-23.

What event (that took place outside the prison) caused Pharaoh to elevate the cupbearer?

The cupbearer and baker's dreams happened three days before Pharaoh threw a big birthday bash for himself. The planning of the party must have made him think about the two officials he'd thrown in prison, the ones whose jobs revolved around feasting. We don't know why Pharaoh restored the one and not the other, but it's important for us to know that while God was interpreting dreams for Joseph in prison, He was also working outside the prison. We can't always see what God is doing, but, like Joseph, we can choose to be faithful where we are and trust Him.

This life is not without evil. We were never promised a road without suffering, in fact Jesus assures us that suffering is part of what comes with the sacred call of being one of His followers. "I have told you these things," Jesus says, "so that in me you may have peace. You will have suffering in this world. Be courageous! I have conquered the world" (John 16:33).

Day 4
DELIVERANCE
Genesis 41:1-16

Before you begin reading chapter 41 today, look back at verse 40:23. Since today's passage is one of hope and deliverance I don't want you to forget how hopeless the situation seemed to be.

The cupbearer failed Joseph. The narrator describes this single failing in two ways. Write them in your journal or in the margin.

RESPOND: How does this double emphasis describe the total failure of human help in this situation?

Just for the record, I don't think it was wrong for Joseph to plead with the cupbearer to help him. He had a connection to the cupbearer and leaned on that relationship in hopes that the cupbearer could plead Joseph's case to Pharaoh. This feels like wisdom to me. Just because the cupbearer failed Joseph doesn't mean he was wrong for asking. It does, however, remind me of human frailty and selfishness, and it makes me think of a few of my favorite verses in the Book of Psalms that describe God's all-sufficient power against the utter limitations of human beings.

> *It is better to take refuge in the L*ord *than to trust in humanity. It is better to take refuge in the L*ord *than to trust in nobles.*
>
> Psalm 118:8-9

> *Do not trust in nobles, in a son of man, who cannot save. When his breath leaves him, he returns to the ground; on that day his plans die. Happy is the one whose help is the God of Jacob, whose hope is in the L*ord *his God.*
>
> Psalm 146:3-5

> *He is not impressed by the strength of a horse; he does not value the power of a warrior. The L*ord *values those who fear him, those who put their hope in his faithful love.*
>
> Psalm 147:10-11

People will fail us for a multitude of reasons. Sometimes their failures are a result of the evil in their hearts and other times it's simply due to the limitations that are inherent to being human.

NOW WE'RE READY FOR THE PINNACLE OF CHAPTER 41.
READ GENESIS 41:1-16.

For how many years had the cupbearer been out of prison and forgotten Joseph?

Those days and months must have crawled by for Joseph, but God never left him, nor did God stop working on Joseph's behalf. An ancient midrash (commentary on the Scripture) describes the cupbearer's forgetting Joseph from God's perspective, "You may have forgotten him [Joseph], but I have not forgotten him."[6]

Paraphrase Pharaoh's dreams in the columns below:

COWS FROM THE NILE	HEADS OF GRAIN

PERSONAL REFLECTION
Is there a person you're continually hoping will be your savior? Reflect on these verses from the psalms. Confess this idolatry to the Lord. Jesus will never forget you.

LOOK BACK AT VERSE 8.

What two groups of people were responsible for hearing and interpreting dreams?

Once Pharaoh told these men his dreams, who precisely was able to help him?

In Egyptian culture, the magicians were trained to interpret dreams. The wise men were well-educated advisors who additionally offered guidance to Pharaoh as ones who were helped by the gods.[7]

While the cupbearer and baker were distressed that none of the dream experts were around to help them interpret their dreams, Pharaoh had every one of them at his disposal! Still, they were incapable. Only the one true God with whom Joseph had an intimate relationship would be able to provide Pharaoh with an answer.

Why did the cupbearer suddenly remember Joseph?

How did Joseph's prior ministry to the cupbearer suddenly play a significant role in Joseph's deliverance?

Maybe you've been serving others for a long time with no outward signs of appreciation. God is not unjust; He will not forget your love. Maybe you've been helping others in your own season of hurt. Perhaps you wonder if your sacrifice is making any difference at all. God is not unjust; He will not forget your love.

I NEVER TIRE OF READING GENESIS 41:14.

What outward changes did Joseph make?

Describe the pace at which Joseph was brought from the dungeon.

The Hebrew word for *quickly* in verse 14 is derived from the root word for *run*.[8] Suffering can be long but deliverance is often quick. Even though God operates outside of time, I have to believe that God, in His great love for Joseph, had been looking forward to this moment when Joseph's suffering in prison would end in an instant. The trying season had dissolved into deliverance, and it was time for Joseph to do what God had been preparing him for all along.

READ 1 PETER 1:3-9.

Peter, a disciple of Jesus Christ, wrote those words. He suffered a great deal as a result of following Christ. What are some of the reasons Peter says we'll experience trials?

According to verse 7, what will be the result of our suffering as followers of Christ? How does this help you rejoice in your trials?

Sometimes a change in perspective is more powerful than the change we hope for in our circumstances. If we see our trials as curses, punishments, or signs of God's displeasure with us, we'll be in a double heap of pain. But if we, like Peter, see our suffering as the crucible by which our faith in Jesus Christ will prove genuine and bring Him glory, well, that is altogether hopeful.

Joseph changed his clothes, signaling a fresh start and a new beginning. Today, let's take off the clothes of self-wallowing, self-centeredness, and despair. Let's choose to focus on the truth that God will not waste a moment of our pain or waiting. He's preparing us for what He's prepared for us.

Day 5
REFRAMING YOUR INADEQUACY
Genesis 41:17-36

When I was in my late twenties, I desperately wanted it to be my turn—to sing, write, teach, have success, be financially stable, you name it. What would have helped me during those years was a deeper confidence that God was preparing me during the waiting, an understanding that all those long years were leading somewhere. You may be waiting for it to be your turn, too. (Each of us is in some stage of waiting.) As we continue to study Joseph's life, I hope it's increasingly clear to you that it's in the waiting God prepares us for what He has for us in the future. So when it's our turn, we'll be ready. Today it's Joseph's turn.

READ GENESIS 41:15-36 AS A REMINDER OF THE CONTEXT.

RESPOND: How had Joseph's waiting and preparation actually qualified him to answer Pharaoh's impossible request?

The Egyptian magicians were expected to hear a dream and be able to interpret it. How did Joseph see his qualifications as being very different from that (v. 16)?

Joseph's response, "I am not able to" (CSB) (or "I cannot do it" [NIV] or "It is not in me" [ESV]) is a single word in Hebrew, *bil'aday*.[9] In one word he summed up the concept we've all felt when faced with someone else's impossible situation: *I don't have what it takes.* Don't you wish we had this single word in English? Think of how much less talking we'd have to do. Joseph's response is absolutely remarkable. He is lightning quick to set Pharaoh's expectations straight: without God, Joseph has nothing for Pharaoh.

LOOK UP 2 CORINTHIANS 3:4-6.

In what ways do you see Paul's words resemble Joseph's response to Pharaoh?

I keep returning to Joseph's response, as well as to the 2 Corinthians passage because I feel especially inadequate right now. To name a few examples, I have some friends who practice a religion that's very different from following Christ, and I don't always know how to talk with them about the good news of Jesus. I have a family member who's suffering from a chronic illness, and several other situations have piled up beyond what I'm able to handle. I keep going back to, if Christ doesn't do it in me or for me, I've got nothing.

Joseph was quick to explain to Pharaoh that he wasn't able to interpret dreams, however, he knew the God who could interpret them.

In yesterday's study you detailed Pharaoh's two dreams. Now I want you to explain the symbolism and its meaning. (See Gen. 41:25-36.)

COWS FROM THE NILE	HEADS OF GRAIN

TRUE/FALSE: The dreams meant two different things.

Why did God give Pharaoh the two dreams? (See vv. 25 and 28.)

**PERSONAL
REFLECTION**

*What God-
given task do
you currently
feel inadequate
to accomplish?
(Think in terms
of standing up for
what's right at
school, sharing
Jesus with a
classmate, being
a leader in the
youth group at
your church,
setting an example
for your friends,
and so on.)*

Pharaoh had all the kingdom's resources in the palm of his hand. He had the magicians and wise men at the snap of his fingers. They had knowledge galore and education for days, but they were missing what the young, Hebrew slave possessed: God-given wisdom.

Detail the wise instruction for handling the coming seven years of abundance and seven years of famine (vv. 33-36).

Juxtaposed against the good and healthy cows, scholar John H. Sailhamer points out that Pharaoh's dreams tie into one of the central themes of Genesis, the knowledge of good and evil.[10] "Joseph is the embodiment of the ideal that true wisdom, the ability to discern between 'good and evil,' comes only from God."[11]

How do you know when it's right to stand with the opinions of the day, and when it's not OK? (Try not to give a "Sunday School answer.")

It's easy to get confused in a culture that frequently changes its opinion about what is good and what is evil—for better or worse. We're often faced with situations that are so complicated we don't know when helping is beneficial or when helping is hurting. How we need the Holy Spirit who not only helps us discern between good and evil, but also gives us the wisdom to overcome evil with good.

Read James 1:5-6. How do we as believers get wisdom?

Read Proverbs 9:10. Where does wisdom begin?

Read Proverbs 2:1-6. The author of Proverbs tells us to seek for wisdom as though it's _____.

RESPOND: Earlier I asked you what God-given task you feel inadequate to handle. Based on Joseph's story and the additional passages of Scripture we've turned to today, how can you reframe your inadequacy as an opportunity to depend on Jesus? Write a prayer of response below.

Today we saw how aware Joseph was of his limitations. Perhaps it's made you aware of your own. The Lord has recently allowed me to go through a long stretch of running up against my limitations, and it's been a humbling season to say the least. It's also been a time of healing. The more I see how incapable I am in my own strength, the more I'm moved by Jesus' delight in still desiring to use me. His tenderness in wanting me to be dependent upon Him has been restorative for my soul. In Joseph's words, I cannot, but God is able. If this is true for Joseph, how true it is for you and me.

SESSION THREE VIEWER GUIDE

FAITHFUL IN BROKENNESS

Fill in the blanks as you're watching the Session 3 video. If you miss any blanks, your leader should be able to help and go over these with you.

1. Don't let _suffering_ lead to sinning.

2. Don't miss the display of God's _kindness_ in the midst of your _suffering_.

3. Suffering makes us fit for the dreams God has for us.

4. You won't serve God more in the _palace_ (good times) than you're willing to serve Him in the _prison_ (hard times).

5. People who _fail us_ can't prevent God's plan for us.

NOTES

- THE LORD WAS WITH JOSEPH ♥
- GOD IS PURIFYING JOSEPH; PUTTING HIM THROUGH THE FIRE TO COME OUT PURIFIED ♥
- GOD IS MAKING US FIT FOR THE CALLING ON OUR LIVES ♥
- WE NEED TO PAY ATTENTION TO OUR ASSIGNMENTS, EVEN THROUGH OUR HARDSHIPS. ♥
- GOD ALWAYS PROVIDES ♥
COLOSSIANS 3:12-16

GROUP DISCUSSION

✢ Is your relationship with the Lord deep enough that sinning against Him actually matters to you? *Yes. All the time, every time.*

✢ Have you ever been aware that the Lord was with you like He was with Joseph? *Maybe not aware, but hopeful that He might be.*

✢ Has God given you an assignment that you didn't like or that you didn't feel like you were good enough for? *Not one that I could point out that God specifically gave me.*

✢ Do you know someone who is distraught right now? How can we help those who are feeling distraught and need someone to listen to, encourage, and serve them? *Yes, my friend Kaylee. By listening to them, encouraging them, and serving them.*

✢ What is God revealing to you today? If there's a temptation you need to flee from, take a page out of Joseph's book and run for your life in the other direction, even if it means leaving something important behind. Let a trusted friend or adult know about your struggle, or ask someone who loves you to keep you accountable. *I think God is bringing a memory back to me for a reason. I just wish that I knew why.*

✢ How does God's faithfulness encourage you to continue to love and serve others even in the midst of your own difficulties? *Because it makes me see the difference God makes in others and I want that difference to be made in me.*

✢ How do you see God using your current trial to prepare you for what's ahead? You may not be able to make out all the details, but think about the ways He's making you more like Jesus. *I think God might be preparing me to leave my family to go and live my dream. I'm nervous, but I think that God might be preparing me for it.*

FAITHFUL IN ABUNDANCE

Joseph's hardships were making him fit for the dreams God had for him. To be a ruler in God's economy first meant a stretch of humbling. It also meant building up perseverance's muscles. And, above all, it meant finding God faithful when no one else was. Before Joseph could lead a people or save a nation He had to know—to be convinced of—the all-sufficiency of God's presence with Him.

When I first moved to Nashville, my sincere aim was to be a wildly successful singer/songwriter all for the glory of God. (If you haven't heard, things didn't play by my script). I was pleased to live for the renown of Christ so much as my own fame had solid footing on His stage. Besides the fact that these two goals were directly at odds with one another, I had also somehow missed Jesus's words about the greatest person being the one who serves (Matt. 23:11).

Looking back, I can see my own Nashville wilderness experience—a barren land for many a musician and performer—as God's training ground for what lay ahead. It was a lonely, walls-pressing-in season of life and for reasons far beyond lost record deals. I didn't know it at the time but God was preparing me to study His Word and impart it to people through writing and speaking, along with a little singing. I couldn't properly do these things without first being humbled. (If it were grammatically acceptable I'd capitalize the "H," because lowercase humbled just doesn't emote enough under the circumstances.) How could I teach the Bible if I hadn't first clung to its pages as if it were a life preserver keeping me afloat? What would I have to say about Jesus if I hadn't yet walked with Him through my own rivers and fires? And how would I know where I was headed in ministry if I didn't grasp the reality that leading through serving is God's upside down way? These discoveries don't usually come to us on a silver platter. Ease doesn't typically sanctify a person.

As we consider Joseph's rise to power we'll notice that His rule will be one of rescue, kindness, and deliverance. He will leverage his influence to sustain lives. If Joseph's heart hadn't been refined in the prison, I don't think he could have reflected the heart of Christ so clearly in the palace. I don't know what future plans God is readying you for, but arriving wherever you're going looking more like Jesus is a destination in and of itself. As we experience this sanctifying transformation, we'll begin to realize that wherever we're headed isn't nearly as thrilling as reflecting Him when we get there.

Day 1

GOD'S SPIRIT IN YOU

Genesis 41:37-45

Every year I spend a week in the Amazon jungle at Justice & Mercy International's Annual Jungle Pastor's Conference. More than one hundred native pastors and their wives attend, my personal heroes who are devoted to reaching the people who live along the river with the gospel of Jesus Christ. We spend several days together learning, worshiping, fellowshiping, and eating. No group of people in the world remind me more of Joseph's dependence on the Spirit of God than my dear friends in the Amazon.

READ GENESIS 41:37-45. AS YOU READ, REFLECT ON THE HOPE AND TRANSFORMATION GOD IS BRINGING ABOUT IN JOSEPH'S LIFE.

When Pharaoh promoted Joseph, several things noticeably changed. Each change points us back to a counterpart from Joseph's earlier days. Draw a line between the corresponding descriptions based on verses 40-44.

JOSEPH THEN	JOSEPH NOW
Receiving the colorful coat	*Second-in-command*
His garment left with Potiphar's wife	*Receiving the signet ring and gold chain*
Rode on Ishmaelite camels	*Rode in Pharaoh's chariot*
Slave	*Fine garments given by Pharaoh*
At the mercy of his brothers	*All of Egypt at his mercy*

Joseph likely shaved his facial hair and his head when he was called from prison (Gen. 41:14) in accordance with Egyptian customs at the time. Ironically, Hebrews generally only shaved their heads as it related to difficult or painful circumstances. Joseph receiving an extra change of clothing represents his transition from impoverished slave to a person of position. In this Egyptian culture, only the royal house and the wealthy would have an additional change of clothes, such as this.[1]

RESPOND: How does this intricate and remarkable turn of events in Joseph's life encourage you to trust God and walk in obedience, even when life is hard and doesn't make sense? Be specific.

LOOK BACK AT VERSES 37-38.

What distinguished Joseph from everyone else at Pharaoh's disposal (v. 38)?

Pharaoh had the smartest and most educated people at his disposal, along with all his kingdom's resources, yet it was the Hebrew slave Joseph who had the one thing no one else in Egypt had—the Spirit of the living God! The Holy Spirit is right now looking for teenagers through whom He can bring the message of reconciliation to the people in our spheres of influence (2 Cor. 5:18-19).

Sometimes I don't connect the power and presence of the Holy Spirit to the circumstances of my everyday life. Instead of relying on Him, I can easily fall back on my resources. I imagine it can be this way for you, too. So today let's do a refresher study on the Holy Spirit and how He operates in our lives. I've chosen all New Testament passages because I want us to see that since Jesus' coming we now have even greater access to God's Spirit.

READ JOHN 14:15-17,25-26.

In verse 16, Jesus gives the Holy Spirit a special name. What is it?

In verse 17, Jesus describes the Holy Spirit as the Spirit of

_____.

NOW TURN TO 1 CORINTHIANS 6:19-20.

In Jewish culture the temple had always been the place of God's dwelling. Now, because of Jesus, the Holy Spirit has taken up residence within you. Don't pass over this reality.

How will this knowledge affect how you treat and use your body today?

READ ROMANS 8:5-6.

What consumes your thoughts? Are they filled with jealousy, materialism, unforgiveness, or comparison thinking? Or are you caught up with the things of the Spirit that promote peace, joy, compassion, kindness, and gentleness? When we purpose to set our minds on the things of the Spirit, we'll naturally walk in accordance with Him.

PERSONAL REFLECTION

Considering the attributes of the Holy Spirit just mentioned, how might you be suppressing His work in your heart?

READ ROMANS 5:5.

What does the Holy Spirit pour into our hearts?

> *God's anger*   *God's peace*
>
> *God's love*   *God's condemnation*

AND FINALLY, LET'S LOOK AT LUKE 11:11-13.

What does this passage tell us about God's desire to give us His Holy Spirit?

Great job working your way through these passages. I needed the reminder, and I hope you did, too. As we close, let's turn our attention back to Joseph's story.

RE-READ GENESIS 41:37-39.

What caused Pharaoh to respond by saying, "Can we find anyone like this, a man who has God's spirit in him?" (v. 38)

As Christ followers, the wisdom given us by the Holy Spirit should have a practical effect on those around us. Whether we're encouraging someone who's in a difficult situation similar to one we've experienced, visiting the sick, giving to the poor, or sacrificing for a loved one, the Holy Spirit in our lives should be tangibly evident to the people around us.

The world is desperately seeking girls with the living God inside them! This is exactly what we, as Christ followers, have to offer a world that's desperate for the Bread of life in a land of famine. Let's commit to talking and praying about what the Lord is asking us to do. Because you—yes, you—have the Spirit of the living God in you.

Day 2
THE GOOD YEARS
Genesis 41:46-52

When Pharaoh pulled a young Hebrew slave from the prison, he did so because Joseph possessed the one thing that no one else in Pharaoh's court had—the Spirit of the living God. The Spirit of God working through Joseph was never supposed to be a phenomenon unique to Joseph in that one brief slice of history. If Joseph was able to bring divine revelation, profound discernment, and godly wisdom to the people of Egypt, how much more should we be able to bring the gospel of Jesus to those around us through the power of the Spirit?

RESPOND: Before we get into today's reading, what specifically stood out to you in yesterday's personal study about the Holy Spirit's role in your life?

So Joseph stored up grain in such abundance— like the sand of the sea—that he stopped measuring it because it was beyond measure.

GENESIS 41:49

READ GENESIS 41:46-52.

How old was Joseph when he entered Pharaoh's service?

According to Genesis 37:2, how old was Joseph around the time of his prophetic dreams? Based on this information, approximately how long had Joseph been in Egypt?

What must it have been like for Joseph as he rode freely across Egypt's vast and open landscape after having been confined at least two years in a prison? Joseph's faithfulness in both places reminds me that we won't serve God in the good times (the palace) if we're not willing to serve Him in the hard times (the prison). It's just the truth. Joseph was faithful to God in his times of waiting and trial, and now he could be entrusted to lead a nation during abundant prosperity.

RESPOND: Whether in a trying season or place of abundance, what does being faithful to God look like for you right now? Be specific.

We often think about how difficult it is to manage our lives during adversity. But it's easy to forget that this can also be challenging in times of surplus and prosperity, too. We can't forget that with seasons of peace, prosperity, and abundance come a wonderful responsibility to steward those blessings.

Look back at Genesis 41:34-35. How are the seven years described in verse 34?

What was required of Joseph during those good years?

TO GIVE US A BETTER PICTURE OF JUST HOW ABUNDANT THESE SEVEN GOOD YEARS WERE, LOOK BACK AT GENESIS 41:49.

Why did Joseph stop measuring the grain he'd harvested?

PERSONAL
REFLECTION

Whether in a trying season or place of abundance, what does being faithful to God look like for you right now? Be specific.

I love this imagery. The harvest was so vast, the grain heaped so high, that Joseph gave up even trying to measure it. I can't help but think of Paul's words in Ephesians 3:20-21, "Now to him who is able to do *immeasurably* more than all we ask or imagine, according to his power that is at work within us, to him be glory in the church and in Christ Jesus throughout all generations, for ever and ever! Amen" (NIV, *emphasis mine*).

An immeasurable amount of grain wasn't the only way God blessed Egypt and prospered Joseph. Let's turn our attention to the dramatic happening in today's Scripture reading, the two sons born to Joseph and his wife, Asenath.

Write the meaning of the names Joseph gave his sons below (vv. 51-52).

Manasseh:

Ephraim:

RESPOND: We'll examine Manasseh's name first. What do you think Joseph meant when he said that God had made him forget his previous hardship and his family/father's household? (Keep in mind: if Joseph's dreams are to be fulfilled, it will entail his father and brothers bowing before him.)

Of course, we know that Joseph hadn't literally forgotten his family or his father. He also hadn't forgotten being thrown in a pit by his brothers, sold, enslaved in Egypt, or left in a prison. Did Joseph figure that having Manasseh was God's new plan, and it somehow replaced the old dream that included his fathers and brothers? We don't know exactly what Joseph was thinking, but it's worth pondering, especially in light of how our own faith and belief can waver in long times of waiting. (See Ps. 27:13-14; Isa. 64:4.)

Now let's consider Ephraim. What two ideas don't seem to go together when it comes to the meaning of his name?

LOOK UP PSALM 126. IT'S A BRIEF PSALM SO READ ALL SIX VERSES ABOUT THE ISRAELITES BEING BROUGHT BACK TO JERUSALEM FROM CAPTIVITY.

RESPOND: Manasseh and Ephraim are both Hebrew names. Why might Joseph have given sons Hebrew names instead of Egyptian ones? (Does this tell you anything about what Joseph still believed God could do with his story?)

PERSONAL REFLECTION

When God pours out His blessing, why do you think He often goes above and beyond our human ability to measure it?

We'll come back to the significance of Manasseh and Ephraim later in our study. Both will play important roles as part of the twelve tribes of Israel and God's redemptive plan throughout the world. The blessing Joseph's sons would be to him and the ways God would multiply them would, much like the grain in Egypt, be perfectly immeasurable. In the meantime, remember that God is able to prosper you in the place of your pain.

Day 3
THE POWER OF GOOD
Genesis 41:53-57

We are figuratively making a cross-cultural journey every time we open our Bibles. When we read Scripture, we often find ourselves in different lands with unfamiliar customs and languages, worlds far away from our own. Today we find Joseph in another situation that's foreign to most of us—famine. The closest I've ever been to a famine is walking to the grocery store in a snowstorm only to find the milk and bread shelves bare.

As we begin today's reading, let's do our best to imagine the desperation these seven years of famine brought about in Joseph's day and also to remember that countless people around the world are currently facing a similar reality today.

READ GENESIS 41:53-57.

When the inhabitants of Egypt cried out to Pharaoh for help he sent them to Joseph with what specific instruction?

RESPOND: Why do you think Pharaoh was so drawn to Joseph? Why was he so trusting of Joseph's plan to save Egypt?

Today's passage is important as it pertains to God's covenant with Abraham.

TURN TO GALATIANS 3:8-9 TO REVISIT THE NATURE OF THE COVENANT.

Who specifically will be blessed through Abraham? (Circle below.)

    Israel   *Europe*   *America*   *All Nations*

How do you see this principle already playing out in Joseph's story?

Pharaoh's trust in Joseph both fascinates and challenges me. How often do we see people of no faith or people of a distinctly non-Christian faith, lean on us, as Christ followers, for wisdom or trusting us for help? It seems the louder narrative is one of Christians and non-Christians facing off in a culture war. Certainly strong disagreements are unavoidable at times, but the principle of God's goodness working through His people to bless unbelievers is still very much part of His plan.

LOOK UP GALATIANS 6:9-10.

To whom are we to do good?

Let us not get tired of doing good, for we will reap at the proper time if we don't give up. Therefore, as we have opportunity, let us work for the good of all, especially for those who belong to the household of faith.

GALATIANS 6:9-10

Notice that Joseph wasn't swallowed up by the Egyptian pagan culture, and neither did he rail against it. Instead he brought the wisdom and goodness of the one, true God to a people who didn't yet know Him. We are to do the same—infiltrating the world with salt that preserves, and light that shines the way. And while the good news of Jesus may, at times, put us in opposition to those who resist Him, we are called to love even those who persecute us.

I want you to see this truth from Jesus' perspective. Matthew 5-7 records Jesus' Sermon on the Mount, where He speaks to a handful of His disciples and a crowd of people who are listening in. Here we get a taste of what it means to live as Christ followers in His kingdom.

READ MATTHEW 5:13-16.

What two metaphors does Jesus use to describe the effect His disciples will have on the world?

Write down everything you know about the purposes of salt and light below:

Salt:

Light:

What does Jesus say will happen if we lose our saltiness?

What specifically does Jesus say our light will bring attention to (v. 16)? (Circle the best answer below.)

Good works   Critical spirits   Self-righteousness   Love

As a result, to whom will the watching world give glory (v. 16)?

When I think of salt in the American South, I think of the vast amounts we use in our foods. But salt is also used for healing wounds, cleansing bacteria, and ridding fabric of stains. Perhaps the most significant use in Jesus' day was the way it was used as a preservative. Since no one had a refrigerator in the first century, salt was rubbed into meats and fish as a way of maintaining their freshness. Jesus' metaphor is clear: we're to be salt that slows down the decay of this world.

RETURN TO TODAY'S TEXT AND READ GENESIS 41:56-57 AGAIN.

How is Joseph acting as salt in the way we just talked about?

LOOK BACK AT GENESIS 40:8 AND 41:16.

How did Joseph shine a light toward God in these two verses?

PERSONAL REFLECTION

How does the concept of being salt and light in the world differ from separating ourselves to the point of having no impact at all?

When Jesus told His disciples in Matthew 5 about being the light of the world, He didn't tell them to go create light. He simply said, "You are the light..." (Matt. 5:14a). And because you're the light, don't hide your light. How absolutely silly it would be for you to put your light under a basket. We do this when we cover up our faith or neglect to reflect Jesus in situations and conversations.

Jesus didn't say, "Go manufacture salt." He said, "You are the salt of the earth" (Matt. 5:13a). But just like the light can be covered up, the salt can lose its flavor, it's impact. It seems Jesus was teaching that when we, as believers, blend in with the world, that's when we lose our saltiness— when we try to mix a little of Jesus with a little of the world.

Salt and light are agents of impact. Salt and light give and expend themselves. Salt and light are distinct from their surroundings. More simply put, we're to be separate from the world for the world.

The picture of Joseph flinging open every storehouse in Egypt while the "nations" came to his door is such an earthy, tangible picture of the abundance and availability of the goodness of God. I can hardly stand it. But, of course, this epic picture is only meaningful because the storehouses Joseph flung open overflowed with grain. And the storehouses overflowed with grain because Joseph had the wisdom to store that grain while the harvest was plentiful. And Joseph had the wisdom to store that grain during the abundant years because he was surrendered to the Spirit of God.

Each of us has a storehouse we can open up to the people around us. We have the Spirit of God in us, the most valuable treasure in our storehouses, and our most meaningful offering to others.

RESPOND: What's in your storehouse, and what is God asking you to do with it for the benefit of others and for His glory?

PERSONAL REFLECTION

In what area(s) of your life are you covering up the light of Jesus? In what area(s) have you mixed your love for Jesus with your love for the world?

Day 4
THE FAMILY IS BACK
Genesis 42:1-9

Our family relationships, no matter how close-knit or terribly strained, are complicated because we're intimately attached to one another and because every relationship in a family is interwoven with all the other family relationships. Nothing in a family happens in a vacuum.

I particularly love that the narrative of Joseph's story never strays far from the reality of his family. Even during his twenty years in Egypt, estranged from his brothers and father, you always have the impression that they're never far away, maybe even lurking just around the next page. It's almost as if at any moment they could bust through the front door looking for Joseph's guest room, wondering if there's any seltzer water in the fridge, and if he possibly has a fresh lime to go with it because, boy, it was a long journey.

READ GENESIS 42:1-9.

What significant place had the famine reached?

As we continue to learn new details about Joseph's story, we always want to keep significant events, places, and people that we've discussed previously in mind.

READ GENESIS 17:3-8.

RESPOND: Based on verse 8 in particular, what seems surprising about a famine being in the land of Canaan?

Returning to today's text, how severe was the famine based on Jacob's words in Genesis 42:2?

Genesis 42:3-4 gives us insight into the family division that still plagued Jacob's household. Ten of the brothers were sent down to Egypt, but one was held back.

Who were the mothers of the ten sons that journeyed to Egypt? And who was the mother of the son who was held back. Hint: She was also Joseph's mother. (Go back to page 18 if you need help.)

RESPOND: As you think of the family rivalries, the brothers' deception, and the favoritism that Jacob still showed to Rachel's children, what do you think it will take for redemption to take place?

Based on Jacob's words to his sons in Genesis 42:1, do they appear to have changed much over the past twenty years? Why or why not?

When the ten brothers arrived in Egypt they didn't recognize Joseph. What strikes me about today's scene is that while Joseph's outward change was significant, it's the sanctifying work we know God has done in his heart that's the most miraculous transformation. And yet, how little seems to have changed about the brothers. Even though they'd been living with their father, Jacob, in the land of Canaan, Joseph had been dwelling in the presence of God. And dwelling with the God of promise is far superior to dwelling in the place of promise.

Dear girls, you may be waiting for a difficult circumstance to change, but with Jesus in that place with you, the greater miracle is that you can be changed. Keep seeking the God of promise and leave the place of promise in His hands.

Speaking of promises, when the brothers bowed before Joseph what did Joseph remember (Gen. 42:9)?

The dream that God gave Joseph symbolized all the brothers bowing down to Joseph. Who was missing at this point?

The experience of Joseph's brothers falling to the ground before him resembled his dream closely enough for it to come rushing back to the forefront of his mind. But this wasn't the fulfillment of the dream because not all the brothers were present. However, this experience was a powerful reminder to Joseph that God was still at work, that He hadn't forgotten Joseph, and that God was going to do what He said He would do.

Turn back to the meaning of Manasseh's name in Genesis 41:51. How is this description different than what happened to Joseph in Genesis 42:9?

PERSONAL REFLECTION

Maybe you feel like you're not in the "place of promise" right now. In what ways can you submit to the God of promise, who has the power to change you from the inside out?

Regardless of what exactly Joseph meant by forgetting his family when Manasseh was born, he couldn't have possibly imagined the scene that was taking place before him.

RESPOND: Is there anyone you haven't forgiven but know you need to? Take some time to put this before the Lord and ask Him to lead you in forgiving that person.

Sometimes it's wise to "forget" certain parts of our pasts, never again to look back. This is especially true if you and the Lord have already dealt with past times of darkness or sin. I'm a big believer in not revisiting what God has taken great pains to deliver us from. That said, other times we can be guilty of running from that which God wants to redeem. Sometimes He wants to bring healing and reconciliation to something that's still broken, and this may require an encounter with our pasts.

I know what you're thinking, *how do I know which is which?* The first answer is, the Holy Spirit, God's Word, and the counsel of trusted believers will help you discern the difference. The second answer is that if you can see hearts softening to the redemptive work of Christ, and if there's an opportunity for further forgiveness and restoration, God may be calling you to face something from your past so He can redeem it.

While the author is speaking of God's loving discipline in our lives, I think the picture of healing is a good note for us to end on.

Day 5

A CAUTIOUS REUNION

Genesis 42:10-20

We ended yesterday's study focusing on forgiveness, especially as it relates to people from our pasts. Forgiveness is essential to a relationship with Jesus Christ. When we experience Jesus' astounding and inexhaustible forgiveness, we will want to forgive others, even if for a time we squirm and struggle through the process.

That said, sometimes we confuse forgiveness with restored relationship. While forgiveness can lead to restoration, forgiveness doesn't require it. In addition, forgiveness isn't synonymous with suddenly having to be best friends with an abusive ex-boyfriend or letting a wildly unhealthy person back into our lives as the boss. Over the next few chapters we'll get a clearer picture of what forgiveness is and also what it isn't. My prayer is that none of us will stop short of forgiving fully from the heart, but also for us not to turn forgiveness into something God never intended it to be.

READ GENESIS 42:7-22.

How did Joseph speak to his brothers when seeing them for the first time in twenty years? (Circle your answer below.)

Tenderly   Harshly   Religiously   Amiably

TRUE/FALSE: *Joseph treated his brothers like family (Gen. 42:7).*

RESPOND: When Joseph first noticed that his brother Benjamin was missing, what might he have thought happened to Benjamin based on his own experience?

After Joseph asked his brothers where they had come from, a series of short exchanges followed, each one revealing important information. In the section below, detail what Joseph discovered from his brothers through each exchange.

JOSEPH	TEN BROTHERS
v. 7: Where do you come from? _____	*From* _____ *to buy*
v. 9: You are spies!	*v. 11: We are all sons of one* _____. *We are* _____.
v. 12: You've come to see the weakness of the land.	*v. 13: We were* _____ *brothers.* *The* _____ *is now with our father.* *One is no longer* _____.

How did Joseph's scheme give him the best shot at seeing his only full-brother, Benjamin, again and most likely his father, Jacob?

While Joseph knew his brothers weren't spies and were clearly in Egypt to buy grain, what he didn't know was whether their hearts had changed. Had they done the same thing to Benjamin that they had done to him? Would they leave one brother to die in prison? Were they still deceitful and ruthless? Joseph was going to find out by devising a plan to test their integrity. Nine of them would be imprisoned and one would be released to retrieve Benjamin.

After holding the ten brothers in prison for three days how did Joseph significantly alter his plan (vv. 18-20)? On the third day, who did Joseph say he feared/revered?

We're not told why Joseph changed his plan from detaining nine brothers and releasing one to releasing nine and detaining one. I personally believe that while God was working on Joseph's brothers in prison, He was also working in Joseph's heart.

RESPOND: When faced with an emotionally-charged situation, how has stepping back for a few days helped you gain perspective and understand God's will?

I trust Joseph's heart while testing his brothers because the Lord had so thoroughly tested Joseph. Similarly, we can only be trusted to speak into the lives of others when our own character has been tested.

READ GALATIANS 6:1.

What is our disposition supposed to be when confronting someone? What are we supposed to do to make sure we're not tempted in the process?

RESPOND: If you're needing to confront someone who has wronged you or another person, what steps can you take to make sure you're doing it with a humble and loving spirit?

PERSONAL
REFLECTION

Out of the information Joseph has gained about his family so far, what do you think was most significant to him? Why?

You may have to draw firm boundaries, you may have to show tough love, and you may have to see whether or not a loved one passes a test of integrity before entrusting them with more of your heart. This is wisdom. But, we can never compromise gentleness, humility, or love.

We've seen a different side of Joseph this week. While his actions have appeared harsh, I believe he knew that unless his brothers dealt with the sin they'd committed against him, they would never be free. I also believe that by remembering the dreams God had given him, Joseph was compelled to press toward their complete fulfillment. By dealing firmly with his brothers, Joseph would hopefully draw both Benjamin and his beloved father into his presence in the near future. Again, Dr. Sailhamer says it best: "What awaited the brothers was not the 'evil' they intended for Joseph but the 'good' God intended for them through Joseph."[2]

SESSION FOUR VIEWER GUIDE

FAITHFUL IN ABUNDANCE

Fill in the blanks as you're watching the Session 4 video. If you miss any blanks, your leader should be able to help and go over these with you.

1. During the good years, don't forget that the <u>HOLY</u> <u>SPIRIT</u> in you is your most profound gift to the world.

2. During the good years, leverage your gift of influence for <u>ETERNAL</u> <u>PURPOSES</u>.

3. During the good years, be a <u>STOREHOUSE</u> for those who are in hard years.

4. During the good years, <u>don't forget</u> who gave you what you have and who brought you to where you are.

NOTES

* Suffering is long, but deliverance is often quick.
* Pharoah didn't have the spirit of god, but Joseph did

GROUP DISCUSSION

✛ What stood out to you from this session's video?

✛ Is there something that God has called you to do that will require the Holy Spirit in you?

✛ Though Pharaoh seemingly had it all; Joseph had the one thing that Pharaoh did not possess: the Holy Spirit. How is the Holy Spirit in you the most profound gift to the world?

✛ How can you leverage your influence for the eternal purposes of God?

✛ What has God done in your life? How can you reflect on His faithfulness and give Him thanks today?

✛ Consider how God might be calling you to be a blessing and storehouse to others. What resources, time, or talents has God gifted you with that you can use to serve those around you?

✛ Share about how God is already using this study in your life and give thanks to Him for how He's working. Pray that He will help your group grow closer to Him.

Session Five

EXTRAVAGANT MERCY

My plan for dinner was to serve my friends a Bolognese sauce over pasta. Think of it as the best kind of spaghetti sauce. Simple enough. I had the sauce simmering on the stove in one pot while I boiled the water for the rigatoni in another. Then in walked my friend with her box of gluten-free, red lentil fusilli—because, why be fun when you can be boring and healthy? I added an additional saucepan to the stovetop for the fake fusilli. Another dear soul trotted into my kitchen hankering for something entirely different, something with more protein, like quinoa. Onto the stove went pot number four, producing a perfectly bubbling quartet. When my last guest breezed in asking for steamed vegetables, that's when I kindly and very loudly articulated, "I don't have enough saucepans for all you people and your tastes!" (The truth is I barely have enough for my own some days.)

I've been thinking a lot about the ways our modern world allows us to curate our lives down to our specific dietary desires, the filters on our photos, and the types of cream in our coffee—plain, hazelnut, French vanilla, grass fed. We're used to being able to customize our experiences to our exact liking. But I've discovered that being able to customize something is not the same as being able to control it. We're still subject to all the things we can't or don't know how to tame, no matter how tailored our environments.

Last week we left Joseph at the height of success and power—second-in-command to Pharaoh and overseer of all of Egypt. I imagine his position afforded him a variety of customizable luxuries. Yet this week's Scripture passage reveals that despite Joseph's exceptional power, he still had no control over his father and brothers. Joseph could steer his brothers in the right direction, but he couldn't change their hearts. He could attempt to draw his father out of Canaan, but he couldn't force Jacob out. The big things, the eternal things lay in the Lord's hands.

As much as I might I think I'm managing my world by honing my preferences, the truth is I'm fully dependent upon the Lord for everything that really matters to me. This includes the lives of my beloved family and friends, the health of those I pray for, the direction of my ministry, even my own breath. Joseph's hope hung firmly on the God of the universe. It wasn't flimsily hooked to an illusion of control. God honors such hope, both yesterday and today.

Day 1
SEVERE MERCY

Genesis 42:21-35

This week we'll be following God's redemptive plan for Jacob's family in the midst of profound brokenness. Jacob's favoritism of Joseph, the guilt of the brothers, and Joseph's own pain from what they'd done to him will come together into a sea of complex turmoil that would look perfectly insurmountable. The very good news is that God's hand is able to tame any sea, even the relational kind. Only He can humble tumultuous waves into a glassy surface so smooth it will reflect His glory and His alone.

For those of you who find yourselves in difficult family relationships, I pray God will give you hope over the next few weeks as we watch Him restore what appears irreconcilably broken. To be clear, we're not heading toward a Disney® version of everyone living happily ever after in Joseph's castle. (Although I do love a good fairy-tale ending, and I've always wondered what it'd be like to have a butler). Our destination is much better than that. We'll witness God and His covenant with Abraham pressing forward through Jacob's family, consuming every good and bad human action along the way as fuel for His plan of redemption.

No matter the brokenness of your family, no matter how strained those relationships, God is able to bless, hold, and strengthen you. He's also able to accomplish His redemptive plan through you, not just in spite of your suffering, but often because of it (Gen. 49:22-26).

No matter the brokenness of your family, no matter how strained those relationships, God is able to bless, hold, and strengthen you.

READ GENESIS 42:18-26 TO REFRESH YOUR MEMORY FROM WHERE WE LEFT OFF LAST WEEK.

What new information do you discover about Joseph's reaction to his brothers when they threw him in the pit (v. 21)?

How did the brothers interpret the trouble they were experiencing in Egypt (vv. 21-22)?

RESPOND: When bad things happen to you, how do you typically interpret them? Do you see them as judgment from God for some sin you've committed?

The brothers made a connection between their present difficult situation and their past sin against Joseph. *"Obviously,* we are being punished for what we did to our brother," they concluded (v. 21, *emphasis mine*). (Your translation may say, "surely," "truly," or "in truth".) The brothers clearly saw that their actions deserved a consequence and implied that God was bringing judgment against them.

IMPORTANT NOTE BEFORE WE GO FURTHER: Jesus made clear that we're not to automatically interpret the difficulties and suffering in our lives as God's punishment. When Jesus restored the sight of a man who was born blind, His disciples asked Him: "Rabbi, who sinned, this man or his parents, that he was born blind?" Jesus definitively answered, "Neither ... " (John 9:2-3).

While we may think it obvious that the brothers would make a connection between their current circumstances and past sin, we as human beings don't always recognize God's discipline in our lives. Sometimes we don't even recognize our own sin.

According to Genesis 3:5, who is the source of the knowledge of good and evil?

According to the prophecy of Jeremiah 31:33, how do we know God's teaching about all things, including right and wrong?

Only when we see our sin and confess it can we receive forgiveness. The very fact that the brothers were beginning to acknowledge that what they had done to Joseph was horribly wrong was a blessing in itself.

Describe Joseph's reaction when he overheard his brothers talking about what they'd done to him (Gen. 42:24).

RESPOND: Genesis 42:24 is the first of several times the Scripture records Joseph weeping (Gen. 43:30; 45:2,14-15; 46:29; 50:1). What does this tell you about his heart?

After Joseph gained his composure, he had Simeon bound before his brothers' eyes. Simeon was the second oldest of the brothers. It's possible that Joseph was planning to imprison the firstborn, Reuben, but when he overheard Reuben talking about how he had tried to save Joseph, perhaps Joseph was moved and went for the next brother in line.

If the brothers cared anything about Simeon, which remained to be seen, they'd have to come back with Benjamin for Simeon's release. Even if they didn't care about Simeon, Joseph knew that the famine would outlast the grain his brothers were returning home with, so they'd have to come back no matter what. This arrangement ensured that Benjamin would also be brought back with them. Brilliant, if you ask me.

READ GENESIS 42:27-35.

When the brothers found their silver in their sacks they were terrified because it looked as if they'd stolen the grain. How would they explain this to the harsh Egyptian lord (Joseph) when they returned to Egypt to retrieve Simeon? Joseph having the silver returned to the brothers at first appeared to be a generous gift, but the infinitely more valuable gift was how God would use it to further convict their hearts—conviction that would hopefully lead them to repentance.

Jesus made clear that we're not to automatically interpret the difficulties and suffering in our lives as God's punishment.

Look closely at verse 28. Who did the brothers conclude was behind this terrifying turn of events?

We can't miss that behind the brothers' punishment was God's redemptive mercy! God would use something as severe as a famine, Simeon's imprisonment, and a "harsh Egyptian ruler" to woo the brothers back to Himself and ultimately back to a place of provision that would save their lives.

Is God using severe mercy in your life to get your attention? What I love about His character is that the discipline God brings is always for our good and always borne out of love. Since the gift of God's Son, Jesus, we don't have to live under condemnation or a sense of dread. A passage in Acts points to the freedom we have when we repent (turn from our sinful direction and back to the Lord).

READ ACTS 3:19-20.

If you're going through a time of discipline, remember these words from Hebrews 12:6a, "the Lord disciplines the one he loves." I find myself smiling as I write these words, smiling at you, as if you're sitting right here in front of me. God only brings correction and discipline to those He dearly loves—for it is then that our eyes are opened to the sin that destroys us, our hearts opened to the forgiveness that heals us, and our hands opened to the times of refreshment that are on their way.

Day 2
WAITING AND TRUSTING

Genesis 42:36–43:14

As we make our way through Joseph's story, I'm continually impressed by God's providential hand accomplishing His work regardless of what all the people in our story choose to do or not do. Jacob and his sons were still free to make decisions and choices, but God in His incomprehensible sovereignty never lost control. While Joseph and Simeon were in Egypt and the rest of the brothers and their father were all the way back in Canaan, God was fulfilling His promises.

READ GENESIS 42:36–43:14.

According to Genesis 43:7, which two people did Joseph keep asking his brothers about, and why are they significant to the fulfillment of Joseph's dreams? (Look back at Gen. 37:6-10 if you need to refresh your memory.)

PERSONAL REFLECTION

There's a difference between working in accordance with God's plan and frantically trying to "save" His plan. Is there any area in your life where you're trying to manipulate or control an outcome on your own terms?

Theoretically, Joseph should have known without a doubt that both Jacob and Benjamin were still alive since both were essential to the fulfillment of his dreams. However, over twenty years had gone by and Joseph had made an entirely new life apart from his family and Hebrew culture. I wonder if he struggled with his faith the way I sometimes do, sincerely believing certain promises of God while simultaneously thinking, *there's no way.*

Once Joseph realized his father and brother were alive, his desire to see them must have intensified. When our hopes are up they have farther to fall, which is why we sometimes find it easier to give up on a dream altogether rather than keep waiting on God to fulfill His promises.

LOOK BACK AT GENESIS 42:36-38.

Back in Canaan, what did Jacob immediately refuse to let Leah's sons do when discussing a return trip to Egypt?

Jacob has further alienated all of Leah's sons by essentially saying that Joseph and Benjamin were his only true sons. How was Jacob's sin of favoritism—we could possibly say idolatry—working against him right then and against God's redemptive plan?

I suppose it was a good thing that Joseph didn't know all the conversations his father and brothers were having, the ones we've been privy to in today's reading. They probably would have only made him worry. The future of Israel seemed to be resting on the woe-is-me shoulders of Jacob and on the equally unstable shoulders of Reuben and Judah (Gen. 43:3-10).

PERSONAL REFLECTION: How does Joseph's story so far remind you that God is sovereign and working all things together to accomplish His plan, regardless of how humans choose to respond?

And she conceived again, gave birth to a son, and said, "This time I will praise the LORD." Therefore she named him Judah. Then Leah stopped having children.

GENESIS 29:35

Describe the differences between Reuben's and Judah's offers of help should Benjamin not return safely to their father. (See Gen. 42:37; 43:8-9.) Was one more selfless than the other? Why?

Though the change is subtle, Judah was beginning to emerge as the leader of his brothers. His rise to leadership would become increasingly important. You'll recall from Session 2 that Judah was the fourth child born to Leah and Jacob.

IN THE MEANTIME, LOOK BACK AT GENESIS 29:35.

What did Leah say after giving birth to Jacob? Why do you think this is significant?

I don't want us to get ahead of ourselves, but it seems to me at Judah's birth we get a hint that God had significant plans for his life.

READ GENESIS 37:25.

What were the Ishmaelites carrying with them on their camels? How does their cargo inventory compare to the one in Genesis 43:11? List the similarities.

I've always found it fascinating that some of the goods Joseph must have seen, smelled, and maybe even tasted on his way down to Egypt were the very gifts his father and brothers would send him as a peace offering over twenty years later. Jacob hoped these gifts as well as the returned silver would appease this harsh "lord of Egypt" and mercy would be shown to Jacob's family.

We began today's lesson with Jacob's resistance to his sons returning to Egypt with Benjamin. What changed his mind?

According to Genesis 43:14, what did Jacob specifically call God? What did Jacob hope God would grant his sons?

The name, God Almighty, was the name given in relation to the covenant promise God made with Abraham in Genesis 17. I believe Jacob used that name as a way of appealing to that promise, the promise of God to make Abraham into the father of many nations. For the promise to be fulfilled, Jacob's family line would have to survive. And for Jacob's descendants to survive, God would have to show mercy to the family.

While recently reading Psalm 33, I thought of Joseph being in a position to put his trust in God instead of in people or circumstances.

READ PSALM 33:13-22.

From where does salvation not *come (vv. 16-17)?*

The psalmist reminds us that our hope and our strength aren't found in a person. The salvation of Jacob's family didn't rest on Pharaoh, Jacob, Jacob's sons, or even on Joseph. The Lord is the One who rescues from death and, as specifically mentioned in this psalm, famine. Without God's sovereign hand working out His plan, each person's agenda would have failed, including Joseph's.

Surely Joseph wondered if his brothers would ever make it back to Egypt and whether Benjamin would be with them. He probably wondered if his elderly father would ever leave Canaan and come to reside in Egypt. He may have worried that some of his family might not make it through the long journey during a famine. Regardless of Joseph's perspective, it seemed that his dreams were hanging in the balance, determined by the decisions of Joseph's brothers and father, people who were hundreds of miles away. But this couldn't be further from the truth. These life-changing details rested in God's hands.

IN CLOSING, READ 1 PETER 5:6-7.

Throughout today's study we've thought about Joseph having to wait and trust while his father and brothers were back home in Canaan discussing and preparing to return to Egypt. Details were emerging. A larger plan was unfolding.

Our hope and strength aren't found in a person.

Day 3
AN UNSHAKABLE DREAM
Genesis 43:15-26

We're well past the halfway point in our study on the life of Joseph. I want to encourage you to keep going. Starting something is easy but finishing it requires commitment. The fact that you've made it this far tells me without a doubt you can finish strong. Keep setting aside the time for each day's work, and don't worry when you get behind. Catch up when you can. Joseph's story in particular builds upon itself, and you'll find the reward at the end is greater than the sum of its parts.

Yesterday we left Jacob by himself in Canaan, Joseph and Simeon in Egypt, and the rest of Jacob's sons, including Benjamin, about to embark on a journey from Canaan to Egypt. The famine was severe. Jacob was afraid. The brothers were fractured. Joseph was presumably waiting with faithful anticipation—and possibly doubt, if he's anything like me. Despite the uncertainty and frailty of our trials and humanity, the hook upon which we can hang all our hope is God's character—He is good and in full control. We'll continue to see this truth unfold today.

READ GENESIS 43:15-22.

What specifically prompted Joseph to tell his steward to go prepare a meal at his house for his family?

Verse 18 tells us the brothers were afraid when they found out they were being taken to Joseph's house. We know from Egyptian history that men in Joseph's position commonly had holding cells within their homes, so this possibility probably added to their fear.[1]

What specifically were the brothers afraid would happen to them? Write down their list from verse 18.

God was the brothers' Advocate here even though they were guilty.

I have to believe the brothers' long list of fears about what they thought was going to happen to them stemmed directly from what they'd done to Joseph and the guilt they'd never dealt with. This is especially true since we learned on Day 1 of this week that they equated the returned silver with God's punishment (Gen. 42:28).

I resonate with the brothers' terror. Especially when I was younger, I lived in constant fear that God's punishment was either nipping at my heels or right around the corner about to pounce on me. I lived with guilt, some that I shouldn't have carried and some that was rightly mine—I didn't know what to do with either one. Whenever I read about the way the brothers interpreted every good or bad thing that happened to them as the just reward for their sin, I think about the mercy and grace of God that frees us from guilt as a way of life.

RESPOND: Are you living in fear of punishment because of a past sin (or sins) that you've never dealt with? Describe.

Look up 1 John 1:8-9. How are we cleansed from past and present unrighteousness?

According to 1 John 2:1-2, who is our Advocate before the Father when we sin?

RESPOND: How do these passages help you think differently about your sin before God and His remedy for it?

I didn't want to miss an opportunity for us to see Jesus' sacrifice as the means of our cleansing and forgiveness. You can walk in freedom. You no longer have to live in fear like Joseph's brothers (1 John 4:18). Let's return to our story in Genesis.

READ GENESIS 43:23-26.

To the brothers' utter shock, how did Joseph's steward respond to them in verse 23?

To whom did Joseph's Egyptian steward attribute the brothers' returned silver?

God was the brothers' Advocate here even though they were guilty—not of stealing the silver but of much worse, selling their brother. Are we seeing a foreshadowing of Jesus Christ as our ultimate Advocate before the Father?

And it gets even better. We miss this in our English translations, but when the steward tells the brothers, "Don't be afraid" he also said, *šalôm*, or "Peace to you."[2] Verse 23 is so powerful because it shows us a group of clearly guilty, undeserving men go from overwhelming fear to incomprehensible peace. Only God could have caused this impossible transition. Incredible.

RESPOND: Write about a time when God brought you from a place of fear to one of peace. How did He do it? What did you learn? It's good for us to write these reminders down for future remembrance.

You can walk in freedom. You no longer have to live in fear like Joseph's brothers.

I can't imagine what the brothers thought when Joseph's attendant, instead of throwing them in prison, showed them extensive hospitality: water for their feet and feed for their donkeys. I mean, it's one thing to cut them some slack, but let's not go overboard here! Or am I the only one thinking that cynically? This is God's unthinkable kindness in one of its earliest revealed forms in Scripture.

When compared with Genesis 37:20, what makes Genesis 43:26 so significant? Describe below.

I love this part of Joseph's story so much. It reminds me of an unshakable truth for those of us who are sons and daughters of the one true God: No one on earth can shatter a dream whose source is in God. As much as the brothers thought they could destroy Joseph and therefore destroy his dreams, God was the Author and Fulfiller of those dreams. The brothers were no match for the God of Abraham, Isaac, and Jacob. Today we've witnessed eleven brothers bowing down to Joseph, the fulfillment of Joseph's first dream.

Day 4

A LAVISH MEAL

Genesis 43:27-34

Today, we'll continue to keep our eyes on the overarching story God is writing, even as we look at the finer details. As we start our reading, let's pick up one verse from yesterday to set the larger context.

READ GENESIS 43:26-30.

Verses 29-30 describes Joseph weeping again. What caused him to weep here?

Then he said to me, "Write: Blessed are those invited to the marriage feast of the Lamb!" He also said to me, "These words of God are true."

REVELATION 19:9

Benjamin was born before Joseph was sold and sent to Egypt. We can only imagine how dear his baby brother was to Joseph, especially since they were the only two who shared Rachel as their mother. When Joseph saw Benjamin, now as a young man, Joseph was overwhelmed with emotion. Add to that the news that his father was still alive despite the famine, the gift of foods he received from his family that would have reminded him of his childhood days in Canaan, and the fulfillment of his first dream when all his brothers bowed down to him—it was all too much.

RESPOND: You may have pain stemming from a family member or loved one. How does Joseph's example encourage you that, by God's grace, deep love for that person is still possible?

CLOSE OUT THE CHAPTER BY READING GENESIS 43:31-34.

TRUE/FALSE: *The Egyptians ate with the Hebrews because they found sharing a meal together to be an enriching cultural experience.*

We haven't yet discussed what it was like for Joseph to not only live in a foreign land with foreign customs and pagan gods but also in a land in which his culture was detested. Even though Joseph's wisdom and oversight were revered at this time, it seems he was a victim of prejudice and racism in his early days in Egypt. Many years later when God delivered the Israelites out of Egypt, He spoke to His people numerous times about treating foreigners with kindness and generosity.

READ DEUTERONOMY 24:19-22.

At the end of this passage, what specific reason did God give for treating the foreigner with kindness and generosity?

Back to today's text in Genesis. What astonished the brothers, other than the fact that they were sitting at a lavish meal in the lord of Egypt's house? (Note the details of how they were seated.)

Look back at Genesis 43:16. What was served at this meal? Given the famine, why was this so extraordinary?

The Bible is much more compelling when we understand the story God is writing and get involved with His story, instead of trying to extract whatever tidbit applies to us.

I think of how the Israelites, years later, would grumble against God in the wilderness and ask, "Can God spread a table in the wilderness?" (Ps. 78:19, ESV). The answer is, He'd already done it at Joseph's table in Egypt in the middle of a famine. And He'll spread His table again when He invites Christ's bride, His church, to sit down at the marriage feast (Rev. 19:9) of the Lamb. This time not in the wilderness, but in heaven.

The food and wine at Joseph's table came from his personal allotment. We continue to see evidence of his forgiving and sacrificial attitude toward those who had hurt him, an attitude beyond most of our abilities to comprehend.

How was Benjamin's portion different than the other brothers'?

RESPOND: What might be the reason Joseph had the brothers seated according to age and gave Benjamin extra portions?

It appears Joseph served extra portions to Benjamin to see if his brothers would react in anger and jealousy like they had done to him. At least at this point, it seems that they were passing the test.

I want you to make one more fascinating comparison. Look back at Genesis 37:23-25. What did the brothers sit down to do after throwing Joseph into the pit? How did this show the depth of their heartlessness?

Only God could have written this story. Only God could have fulfilled it.

The tragic and horrific treatment of Joseph begins with a meal, and the beginnings of restoration between Joseph and his brothers end with a meal. Instead of the punishment the brothers deserve, they sit down to a lavish feast in the middle of a famine.

God was piecing back together the hopelessly broken relationships of Jacob's twelve sons as they formed a peaceful union around the table. Only God could have written this story. Only God could have fulfilled it. Only God, in the midst of jealousy and hatred, could have brought šalôm.

Day 5
THE SILVER CUP
Genesis 44:1-17

Growing up in church I remember baptism Sundays being some of my favorite services of the year, and this wasn't just because we got out of a sermon. To this day, nothing inspires me more than Christ followers talking about what Jesus has done in their hearts and lives. We're moved by these stories because they remind us that people like you and me, people who are broken and were once in despair, have been profoundly transformed by the person of Jesus. There's simply no other explanation for the dramatic renewal in our lives. I believe today's reading will serve as a reminder that when God is at work, people really can change.

READ GENESIS 44:1-17.

Joseph put his brothers through a third and final test. In the space below or in your journal, summarize this last test you just read about. I described the first two for you.

1. Joseph accused the brothers of being spies, imprisoned Simeon, and demanded the brothers bring Benjamin with them when they returned for more grain (Gen. 42:18-20).
2. The brothers' silver was returned to their sacks, and it appeared they were thieves (Gen. 42:35).
3.

In whose sack was the silver cup found, and why was this significant? List every reason you can think of.

How did the steward's prescribed punishment differ from what the brothers suggested their punishment should be (vv. 9-10)?

The wisdom of God was behind Joseph's masterful tests. Through each of the tests, God was working on the hearts of the brothers, while showing Joseph what kind of men his brothers had become. This last test was perhaps the most significant because it presented the brothers the opportunity to do to Benjamin what they had done to Joseph. "[Joseph] cannot trust himself to them until he knows that they are trustworthy."[3] Now that Benjamin had become the "guilty party," the rest of the brothers were free to abandon him and save themselves. If they still cared nothing about their father's heart and nothing about their half-brother Benjamin, they would sacrifice Benjamin as they sacrificed Joseph.

How did Judah respond on behalf of himself and his brothers (v. 16)?

LOOK BACK AT GENESIS 37:25-28.

Whose idea was it to sell Joseph? (Circle the best answer below.)

Reuben   *Benjamin*   *Simeon*   *Judah*

In what ways had Judah changed, and what brought about these changes?

PERSONAL RESPONSE

Based on what you've read so far, what do you believe this series of tests was designed to accomplish in the brothers' lives?

RESPOND: In Genesis 44:16, Judah says, "How can we plead? How can we justify ourselves? God has exposed your servants' iniquity." Since Judah knew he and the brothers weren't guilty of stealing the silver cup, what sin do you think Judah was talking about here?

Deep within our hearts we know our sin must be paid for and our guilt dealt with.

God was relentless. He wasn't going to stop chasing the brothers until they recognized what they'd done, faced their pasts, and ultimately acknowledged Him. While God's conviction may not feel good in the moment, the fact that He won't let us ignore our sin is, to me, one of His greatest characteristics.

Have you ever been in a situation before the Lord where your thoughts were similar to Judah's: *How can I plead? How can I justify myself? God has exposed my sin!* Maybe you're in that situation right now. This conviction is the kindness of God's Holy Spirit stirring you, pleading with you to turn from your sin and receive forgiveness. Don't resist it; receive it by responding with repentance.

Judah's confessional statement took place thousands of years before the cross of Christ and the unique indwelling of the Holy Spirit (not to mention before the Mosaic law). Still, in Judah's response we sense God's conviction. Deep within our hearts we know our sin must be paid for and our guilt dealt with. Humanity has tried to handle sin in countless ways, but only One has ever been able—and ever will be able—to forgive sin, to relieve guilt, and to wash away shame.

LOOK UP 1 JOHN 4:9-10.

In verse 9, how does John say that God's love was revealed to us?

According to verse 10, what is the ultimate definition of love?

Your translation may say that Jesus was the atoning sacrifice for our sins, or the propitiation. For our purposes, we can simply say that God is a holy God whose wrath must be poured out upon sin, otherwise He wouldn't be a God of justice. All sin must be paid for. Since we, as humans, are guilty sinners and unable to pay for our own sin, God sent His Son, Jesus Christ, to absorb God's wrath on our behalf. Jesus substituted His life for our lives. The apostle Paul in 2 Corinthians 5:21 says, "He made the one who did not know sin to be sin for us, so that in him we might become the righteousness of God."

If you've gone through this study without having pulled its thread of redemption straight into your own heart, will you do so now? Jesus is the Redeemer to whom this whole story points. Judah was willing to take the punishment for himself and his brothers, but Jesus blamelessly took our punishment for us on the cross. And that is just the beginning. Jesus invites us to follow Him through faith and repentance, learn from His teaching, and obey what He says. He gives us new hearts. This is not religious jargon. This is abundant life with Jesus.

LETS RETURN TO GENESIS 44:17.

RESPOND: Judah pleaded for all the brothers to be taken as slaves, not just Benjamin. Why do you think Joseph insisted that only Benjamin be taken as a slave?

PERSONAL RESPONSE

If you want to begin following Jesus, write a prayer of response below or in your journal. Confess your sin, acknowledge that Jesus and Jesus alone has forgiven you because of His death and resurrection, and tell Him you want a relationship with Him.

This is a precarious point in our story. If the brothers didn't pass the test of trying to save Benjamin it appeared all would be lost, for how would Joseph ever be able to trust them? But if they all became Joseph's slaves, what would happen to their father, Jacob, and their families left behind in Canaan, all of whom would starve in the famine? Only God could work this one out.

As we close today, let's contemplate the immense love that God the Father has for us in sending His beloved Son, Jesus, to be our atonement. In the same vein as Judah we cry, *How can we justify ourselves when our sin is ever before us?* The truth is we can't. And that's precisely why Jesus has done it for us.

SESSION FIVE VIEWER GUIDE

EXTRAVAGANT MERCY

Fill in the blanks as you're watching the Session 5 video. If you miss any blanks, your leader should be able to help and go over these with you.

1. Whatever mercy we think our <u>SIN</u> <u>REQUIRES</u>, <u>more</u> is <u>needed</u> and <u>more is</u> always <u>there</u> <u>in Jesus</u>.

2. The mercy Joseph shows to his family as a <u>brother</u> will prove more significant than the mercy he shows to Egypt as a <u>ruler</u>.

3. Sometimes the very thing we resist the most is actually the <u>mercy of God</u> saving our lives.

NOTES

- THE ENTIRE STORY HINGES ON THIS ONE WORD: MERCIFUL ♥
- MERCIFUL: YOU ARE WORTHY OF PUNISHMENT BUT ARE SHOWN KINDNESS ✓
- YOU ARE MEANT TO BE GOD'S EXPRESSION OF MERCY TO THE ~~WORD~~ WORLD ♥

✣ What part of the today's video teaching resonated with you? Why?

MERCY IS THE KEY OF JOSEPH'S STORY

✣ How did the video teaching about the mercy of God toward Jacob's family help you better understand the nature of Jesus' mercy toward us?

FIRST TIME MERCY HAS BEEN MENTIONED

✣ Discuss how you would you define mercy. How has mercy been extended to you in your life.

✣ Have you experienced guilt for an extended period of time? If so, how did it affect your life? Discuss some practical steps you can take to live in the reality of His forgiveness.

✣ Who in your life is God calling you to extend mercy to? Why might you be hesitant to do so?

✣ When have you resisted the Lord's prompting, only to later realize it was the Lord showing you mercy?

✣ What other thoughts or questions do you have so far regarding the teaching or your personal study?

THE PROCESS OF FORGIVENESS

As spring approaches, I'm always anxious to get in my garden to plant tomatoes. I have to be careful about the timing to avoid the chance of a frost after they've been planted. I dig my trenches, lay the plants in a bit sideways, and cover them with soil. The year I started my tomato seeds indoors, all manner of heirloom varieties, it was hard to imagine how these delicate little flakes could transform into something as hearty and substantial as the tomato. But that year I watched them run their race from seed to delicious salad. They sure showed me.

The funny thing about gardening is that you can hover over your plants, stare at them like you're trying to catch them in the act of growing, and never visibly perceive so much as a frame of change. They don't ever appear to be anything but paused. But give them a day or two, maybe a couple of weeks, and vines have shot off in unruly directions with yellow flowers giving way to green orbs. And weeds you didn't even know existed have now taken your vegetables hostage. Growth. Change. Life. It's the way the garden goes. But don't expect to witness a garden's progress in anything but stages. Garden plants won't give up all their secrets of growing and changing, only that they're doing so.

Gardening has taught me about seasons, patience, and persistence. I've learned that even when I can't visibly see it, growth is happening in my own life and in the lives of those around me. When I want to give up on daily obedience to Jesus for lack of visible progress, there lays the garden hoe of faithful study, the pairing sheers of cleansing prayer, and the well-worn gloves for serving others. "And let us not be weary in well doing," the Word says, "for in due season we shall reap if we faint not" (Gal. 6:9, KJV).

I imagine Joseph to be weary at this point in the story. I imagine him wondering if any of his faithful interactions with his brothers have made a difference. The returned silver, the extra grain for their families, a lavish dinner at his table, his private tears—was it all for nothing? Were transformation and reconciliation really possible? Would Egypt's grain be the only harvest Joseph would ever know, or was a crop of reconciled relationships on its way? Hint: When the Master Gardener is at work, and we're laboring beside Him, the harvest may not come on our timetable, but it promises to be plentiful.

Day 1
JUDAH AND TAMAR
Genesis 38

Today we're going to hold our place in chapter 44 and spend the day looking at a significant part of Judah's story in chapter 38. (You may remember, earlier in our study we skipped chapter 38 with the intention of returning to it.) As you've already noticed, Judah was emerging as the leader of the brothers and was taking his place as a significant character in our story. This would continue to be nothing short of shocking, especially since we already know that it was Judah's idea to sell Joseph into slavery. But that's just the half of it. Today we'll look at some other not-so-shiny moments in Judah's life, ones that took place after he sold his own brother into slavery.

This section may feel like a break from Joseph's story, but as we continue to see how God is weaving every detail together, we'll begin to view this larger narrative not as Joseph's story or Judah's story, but as our Redeemer's.

READ GENESIS 38. IT'S A LITTLE LONG, AND IT'S A CRAZY ONE FOR SURE, BUT NO ONE CAN SAY IT'S BORING.

I know what you're thinking. What in the world? How is this even in the Bible? You may have other questions like I do, some of which I hope we'll answer as we go. In the meantime, keep in mind that God can use any person and any circumstance to accomplish His promises. In some ways, I find that the crazier and more corrupt Genesis 38 gets, the more faithful we find God to be. This may not all be clear today, but by the time we finish our study, I hope this truth will be remarkably evident.

Where in the timeline of Joseph's story did Judah leave his homeland and marry a Canaanite woman? (See Gen. 37:36–38:1.)

God is weaving every detail together.

"The fact that the [Judah] narrative seems to lie outside the course of events of the Joseph story shows that the writer has put it here for a special purpose."[1] By inserting this chapter about Judah in the middle of the Joseph narrative, it seems the narrator wants us, as the reader, to juxtapose Judah's story with Joseph's story.

Draw a line to connect each statement to the brother it describes:

Innocent when being sold

Slept with a "prostitute"

Judah

Married an Egyptian who
was given to him

Was forced to leave his
brothers and homeland

Married a Canaanite
by choice

*Judah recognized
them and said,
"She is more in the
right than I."*

GENESIS 38:26

Wouldn't sleep with
Potiphar's wife

Joseph

Honest

Guilty of selling his brother

Dishonest

Left his brothers and
homeland by choice

*Look up Genesis 24:1-3 and 28:1-3. Abraham and Isaac did not
want their sons to marry _____ women. (Circle the best
answer below.)*

Promiscuous   Widowed   Unattractive   Canaanite

The patriarchs wouldn't let their sons intermarry with Canaanite women. This instruction wasn't motivated by racism or elitism. These unions were prohibited because the women of that culture didn't worship the one true God. The people living in the land of Canaan at the time were part of a pagan culture worshiping pagan gods. The Hebrews, on the other hand, were God's chosen people, set apart for His purposes and ultimately for the blessing of the entire world. By intermarrying with Canaanites who didn't worship or serve their God, the Hebrews' purpose as a nation would be compromised.

*Look back at verses 38:11,14. How did Judah deceive Tamar, and
how would this have affected years of her life?*

We can't underestimate the power that Judah held over Tamar. In withholding his third son from her, Judah relegated Tamar to her father's house, without a husband or the prospect of having a husband and without any hope to carry on her family line. Not to mention that Judah betrayed Tamar, having promised his son, Shelah, to her while never intending to follow through.

When Judah found out that Tamar had disguised herself as a prostitute and she was the one he slept with, in what surprising way did he describe her (v. 26)?

I would have expected Judah to acknowledge his sin of sleeping with someone he thought was a prostitute, but what did he confess instead (v. 26)?

PERSONAL RESPONSE

How do you see this same abuse of power mixed with selfishness, deceit, and betrayal in our own culture? Although this story may initially seem far outside of our context, it's more relatable than we think.

I think it's significant that soon after Judah and his brothers sold Joseph into slavery, Judah left his family and homeland. I think it's also significant that he ran straight into the arms of a Canaanite woman. Was he escaping his guilt? Had he hardened his heart and, as a result, chose to plunge further into selfishness and sin? I know firsthand my choices to sin can lead to more sin if I'm not repentant. But the opposite is also true. When I confess my pride, jealousy, selfishness—and I choose obedience, I'm encouraged to walk into further obedience.

The means don't justify the ends, but Tamar's radical commitment to follow God's law and carry on the precious line of Judah will secure her a renowned place in Israelite history.

LOOK BACK AT GENESIS 38:27-30.

Which of Judah and Tamar's twin sons was ultimately born first? (Circle the answer below.)

    Perez   *Zerah*

At the risk of giving too much of the significance of our story away all at once, look up and read Matthew 1:1-3. The firstborn son is found in whose preeminent genealogy?

Reading and writing about evil, betrayal, abuse of power, degradation of a woman's body, and heartbreak never makes for a good day. But our viewpoint broadens if we step back and consider this chapter through the lens of a few thousand years of hindsight. In those years we see God actively keeping His promises, fulfilling His covenant to Abraham, Isaac, and Jacob by bringing twin boys out of a mess of a situation, one of whom would be in the line of Christ. God has been redeeming the undeserving like Judah, Tamar, you and me, all along the way. If we can allow that truth to break through the darkness, then yes, today *is* a good day. A very good day.

God has been redeeming the undeserving like Judah, Tamar, you and me, all along the way.

Day 2
A SUBSTITUTE
Genesis 44:18-34

I'm so glad you're back after yesterday's tour through Genesis 38. That was no small feat. You can now see why there was simply no way we could ignore that little detour in Judah's life, especially since he's taken center stage in Joseph's story. With all of Judah's history in mind— from his mother Leah praising the Lord at his birth, to his part in selling Joseph into slavery, to his rebellious journey from home, to betraying Tamar and sleeping with her, to his twin sons—we pick up with the next part of his story.

READ GENESIS 44:14-29.

In a few sentences, describe the essence of the dilemma that the brothers and their father, Jacob, were in.

In the Christian Standard Bible (CSB), Genesis 44:16a reads, "'What can we say to my lord?' Judah replied. 'How can we plead? How can we justify ourselves? God has exposed your servants' iniquity.'" We looked at this verse on Day 5 of last week, but I want to revisit Judah's language in light of yesterday's study.

How was Judah's disposition in Genesis 44:16 similar to his disposition in Genesis 38:26?

As Judah recounted his story, he shared Jacob's words of lament about Joseph being torn to pieces (Gen. 44:28). Of course Judah couldn't say what really happened to his brother because that would have meant confessing to something immeasurably worse than one of them having stolen Joseph's silver cup. What a convoluted mess Judah and the brothers were in. Even in trying to tell the truth, Judah couldn't tell the whole truth because of his past offenses. And isn't that one of the worst feelings in the world?

How do each of the following verses correlate with the place in which Judah and his brothers find themselves? Write a sentence next to each reference.

Proverbs 14:12

Romans 6:23

Galatians 6:7

God's grace is what shows us our sin in the first place and His grace is what rescues us from it.

While we can't truly ask for forgiveness without first grasping the weight and reality of our sin, God's love doesn't intend to leave us in our sin. As we've already discussed in our study, God's grace is what shows us our sin in the first place and His grace is what rescues us from it. John Newton said it best in "Amazing Grace," "Twas grace that taught my heart to fear, and grace my fears relieved."[2] The tests that Joseph put his brothers through, as a result of God's leading, weren't for the sake of revenge but to lead them to repentance.[3]

Judah and his brothers were coming to grips with the horror of what they'd done to their brother, Joseph, and what they'd done to their father, Jacob, by bereaving him of his beloved son. Joseph's purpose in orchestrating this series of tests wasn't to condemn or destroy his brothers but to lead them to a place of restoration.

READ GENESIS 44:30-34.

How was Judah's attitude toward Benjamin different from his earlier attitude toward Joseph? Why was this significant?

RESPOND: Judah's deep concern for his father Jacob was obvious and compelling. He certainly didn't care about Jacob when he tried to kill his beloved son Joseph years earlier. What do you think brought about this change in Judah?

What did Judah offer to do in verse 33 that proved his heart had significantly changed?

PERSONAL REFLECTION

Can you think of a time when your sin was plainly before you and there was nothing you could do to justify it to God, others, or yourself? How did this deepen your appreciation for Jesus and His sacrifice for you?

I want you to hang on to Genesis 44:33 because it will be important near the end of our study. In the meantime, note that Judah was offering to be a substitute for Benjamin and the brothers. He was offering to stand in the place of their judgment. He was offering to take the penalty of Benjamin's "sin" of stealing the silver cup so everyone else could return home as free men, so their father, Jacob, wouldn't die of heartbreak, and so their families wouldn't die of starvation.

God is using this story to work in our hearts all these years later. Only God can accomplish so many purposes with one story.

Day 3

A STUNNING REVELATION

Genesis 45:1-8

Today's reading needs no introduction, other than to say what you're about to read took place twenty-two years after Joseph last saw his father. Joseph was seventeen years old when God gave him dreams, followed by him being sold into slavery. Then there was a span of thirteen years—some of the time spent in Potiphar's house, some of it in a prison. Joseph was thirty years old when promoted to be Pharaoh's second-in-command, where he spent seven years overseeing the harvest. At the time of our reading, Joseph was two years into overseeing the seven years of famine.

READ GENESIS 45:1-8.

Out of all the moments Joseph could have chosen to reveal himself, why do you think he chose this moment? (Keep Judah's speech from Gen. 44:16-34 in mind)

Far from wanting his brothers to endlessly suffer for what they'd done to him, all this time Joseph had been longing for them do the right thing. When Judah spoke on behalf of himself and his brothers and declared them all guilty before God, when he spoke tenderly about their father, Jacob, and finally, when he offered to be the one to suffer so everyone else could go free, that's when Joseph knew true repentance had taken place. "Judah's plea for Benjamin shows how sincerely they renounce their former sin (44:33–34)."[4]

In this passage, Joseph wept again. What details reveal the extreme nature of his weeping?

What was the first question Joseph asked his brothers after revealing his identity to them, and how did they respond?

There's no way for us to experience the same shock the brothers felt in that moment, partly because we've known all along that this harsh Egyptian lord was their innocent, suffering brother, Joseph. His identity isn't new to us. But pause for a moment and consider the brothers' awe when the man who stood in charge of their fate, this Egyptian ruler, suddenly said to them with bloodshot eyes and a tear-drenched face, "I am Joseph!"

The brothers are described as being *dismayed*, *troubled*, or *terrified* at this news, depending on your translation. The definition of the Hebrew word *ba·hal* means to be " … alarmed, i.e., pertaining to being in a state of great fear, even causing trembling."[5]

RESPOND: Why were the brothers absolutely terrified at Joseph's revelation? Give every reason you can think of.

If we weren't aware of the work God had done in Joseph's heart, we would fully expect the brothers to be terrified in Joseph's presence because we'd fully expect Joseph to repay them for what they'd done. At the very least we would expect Joseph to execute justice.

JOSPEH'S LIFE

17 YEARS OLD
Joseph sold into slavery

30 YEARS OLD
In the service of Pharaoh

39 YEARS OLD
Reveals himself to his brothers, two years into the famine

What specific action did Joseph tell his brothers to take in verse 4? How was his tenderness different from everything we might have expected?

Thousands of years before the coming of Christ we're met here with a scene of forgiveness, reconciliation, love, grace, and affection that casts a gleaming light on the good news of the gospel that will extend to every nation. Joseph was not treating his brothers as their sins deserved.

READ TITUS 3:3-7.

Paul lists specific sinful conditions we can all relate to. According to verses 4-5, what appeared to us in the middle of these conditions?

After Joseph revealed his identity initially, he revealed it a second time with a little extra detail. *I'm Joseph. You know, the brother you used to have, the one you sold into Egypt. Yeah, I'm that guy.*

What reasons did Joseph give for telling his brothers not to be grieved or angry with themselves? (See vv. 5-8.)

PERSONAL REFLECTION

As you consider the greater story of redemption being woven together by the all-knowing God, how might He be accomplishing repentance and redemption in your own heart and story?

RESPOND: Three times in the course of verses 5-8, Joseph stated it was God who had sent him to Egypt. How do you reconcile this statement with the fact that his brothers had sold him into slavery?

Verse 8 is one of a few darts in Scripture that lands straight in the bull's-eye of God's mysterious sovereignty. We'll deal with this idea further when we reach chapter 50. God is able to take whatever good, bad, or indifferent actions people have taken toward you and not merely salvage them, but somehow, in ways we can't understand, orchestrate them for His purposes and your good.

This might be terrifying news if we didn't know, from other parts of the Bible, that God is altogether good, there is no darkness in Him, and He is incapable of evil (Num. 23:19; Ps. 145:9; 1 John 1:5). I can't say I completely grasp how all this fits together. But we'll find out later in our story that God didn't pretend the sin of what the brothers did to Joseph didn't exist or wasn't a big deal.

Who would specifically benefit as a result of Joseph being sent ahead of his family to Egypt? (See v. 7.)

Is anyone else as moved as I am in this moment by the grace of God flowing through Joseph toward his brothers? Joseph had once worn a robe of many colors, now he wore a robe of many Christlike qualities. The first was torn and dipped in blood. The latter would only come about in full because of Christ's torn body and shed blood for us. This grace we received from Christ came while we were still sinners. A grace we didn't deserve. A grace that met us as a result of Jesus' suffering, not our own. This gospel grace that rescued us was foreshadowed by the "great deliverance" Joseph described in his day (v. 7). Now we've experienced an infinitely greater deliverance since Jesus was raised from the dead, having redeemed us from our sin. As God used sinful men like Joseph's brothers to bring about a great deliverance for the Israelites and the whole world, so God used sinful men to put Jesus to death to bring about deliverance for all who would trust and follow Him.

PERSONAL REFLECTION

What are some specific characteristics of a truly repentant heart?

The brothers must have expected Joseph's fury and wrath to be unleashed on them at his revelation. Instead Joseph said those four glorious words, "Please, come near me" (v. 4).

CLOSE TODAY'S STUDY BY READING HEBREWS 10:19-23.

The author of Hebrews tells us that we can _____ in full assurance. (Circle the best answer below.)

Stand back   Fearfully Approach   Tearfully Approach   Draw Near

I hope today's section of Joseph's story has awakened a new affection in you for God, His Son, Jesus, and the salvation He's brought us. A judgment is coming, but we need not fear it if we've been cleansed once and for all by the blood of Jesus shed for us on the cross.

Day 4
A STUNNING REDEMPTION

Genesis 45:9-24

I grew up in an environment where often the message was: Do the right thing, and you'll be blessed. Don't do the right thing, and you'll be punished. As a stand-alone concept this has a measure of truth to it, but it doesn't take grace into account. It doesn't allow for God's love expressed through the person of Jesus to step in and give us what we don't deserve and spare us from what we do deserve.

Today we're going to read about the tangible, everyday grace that showed up with its boots on the ground for an undeserving group of people, Jacob and his sons. There's just no other way to describe the grace we're going to read about other than calling it amazing.

SLOWLY TAKE IN GENESIS 45:9-15 TODAY.

Who continued to be Joseph's focus throughout the famine (vv. 9, 13)?

Cast your burden on the LORD, and he will sustain you; he will never allow the righteous to be shaken.

PSALM 55:22

Joseph wanted his father, Jacob, to know that God had made him "lord of all Egypt" (v. 9). Joseph could have touted his own perseverance, scrappiness, and mental toughness in reaching this powerful position. Instead, he gave glory to God as the only One who could have achieved and pieced his success together.

RESPOND: When we think back on the hard, even impossible, times in our lives that God has redeemed, sometimes we put the focus on our own strength and intellect. In what ways can you specifically give God the glory for the redemption He's brought about in your life?

What part of Egypt did Joseph tell his family they could settle in? (Circle the best answer below.)

Goshen   Dothan   Canaan   Cairo

List everyone and everything Joseph told his brothers to bring back to Egypt with them (v. 10):

Sometimes we forget that our obedience not only affects us but the people around us, even those we might not know. Joseph's surrender and obedience to the Lord throughout these twenty-two years was now working out an incomprehensible salvation for generations of people he'd never even met—in the middle of a devastating famine. Obedience to Christ may not come easy but the blessings are without rival.

Joseph now invited his family to come live near him (v. 10). He told them that he would sustain them (v. 11). Up to this point Joseph protected himself by keeping his brothers at a distance through his knowledge and power over them. But when the right time came, he relinquished these protective measures out of love and care for his family. Joseph's promise in verse 11 uses the word *sustain*, a word used in other parts of Scripture to describe God's care for us.

LOOK UP PSALM 55:22.

What does the psalmist tell us to do so we can experience the sustaining provision of the Lord?

Obedience to Christ may not come easy but the blessings are without rival.

CONTINUE BY READING GENESIS 45:16-24. AS YOU READ, MENTALLY NOTE JOSEPH AND PHARAOH'S DETAILED CARE OF THE BROTHERS, THEIR FAMILIES, AND LIVESTOCK.

The word that immediately came to my mind after reading this section is *lavish*. Pharaoh and Joseph lavishly cared for them—from the invitation for every family member to come to Egypt, to a pastureland for their herds and flocks, to provision from the best of all the land of Egypt during a famine, to enormous wagons that would serve as moving trucks, to changes of clothing, extra silver, gift baskets for Jacob, grain for the journey—all for the undeserving. I'm utterly astounded and not merely at Joseph and Pharaoh's kindness—though it is impressive—but at God's lavish goodness toward Joseph's family. The story just can't be any clearer—this colossal rescue was no one's idea but God's, not to mention His doing.

God's lavish abundance is on display in several areas, but I want to draw our attention to one verse in particular: Genesis 45:18. Here Pharaoh offered Joseph's family the "fat/richness of the land," and this unique expression was used only here in the Bible.[6] In the middle of scarcity, God was able to provide Jacob's family with the finest the land had to offer.

Even though Pharaoh was sending the provision of wagons (moving trucks) with the brothers, the wagons were for the people (v. 19). There was no need to shove the ancient Near Eastern equivalent of grandma's antique chest, their brand new fifty-two inch television, or a their entire closet into the truck. Pharaoh encouraged traveling light and leaving some things behind for the abundance of what was ahead.

Why did Pharaoh tell them not to worry about bringing all their stuff (v. 20)?

Just as Pharaoh told Joseph's brothers not to lament anything they would have to leave behind because the best of the land would be theirs, so Jesus reminds His followers that no matter what we're experiencing, God's abundance is ours in Christ (2 Cor. 1:20; 1 Tim. 6:17; 2 Pet. 1:3). If you're like me, you tend to lament the stuff you can't fit into the wagon—the stuff you've had to leave behind in the course of following Jesus. But what is any of that when the best of all the land, the abundant life in Christ, awaits you?

I believe one of the primary reasons Joseph was able to forgive and show love to his brothers was because He had experienced God's provision and presence in his life. Joseph knew his experience in Egypt wasn't some cosmic accident or the triumph of his brothers' evil. He clearly recognized God's hand in his life, and perhaps he recognized God's work in the grander narrative of keeping His covenant with Abraham and his descendants. Joseph was able to love his brothers because he knew and experienced God's love for himself.

First John 4:10-11 says, "Love consists in this: not that we loved God, but that he loved us and sent his Son to be the atoning sacrifice for our sins. Dear friends, if God loved us in this way, we also must love one another."

Day 5

A GREAT SALVATION

Genesis 45:25–46:27

Have you ever played checkers or chess? I wasn't very good at either of those games—I've always needed a ball in my hands—but what I do know is that checkers involves a lot of quick, reactive moves while chess is more complex and requires strategic forethought. It's playing the short game versus the long game. I am queen of the short game in case you were wondering.

On my bad days, I measure God's favor toward me (or lack thereof) by whatever has gone right or wrong that day. When I do this, I forget that not only is God after the long game in my life—my personal sanctification, spiritual growth, blessing of others, heart growing to look more like Christ's—He's also after His long game. In other words, God cares deeply about our individual lives, and at the same time, He wants to use us in His far bigger story of redemption. We're meant for something much larger than ourselves, but this is easy to forget in our instant gratification and selfie culture.

I bring all this up because we've recently been looking on as Jacob's family members have each made a lot of the individual checker. But today we're about to be astounded and comforted by the long plan God has had from the beginning and is still fulfilling to this day. And, sidenote, it's a plan we get to be part of.

READ GENESIS 45:25-28.

Describe Jacob's two contrasting responses upon hearing the news that Joseph was still alive.

What specifically did Jacob see that convinced him that Joseph was still alive (v. 27)? Circle the best answer below.

    An angel   *Donkeys*   *Benjamin*   *Wagons*

It's important to note Jacob's numbed heart and lack of belief (v. 26) contrasted with his revived heart and belief. I've always loved the picture of the gray-haired, aged, and emotionally-wounded Jacob lifting his head back to life, revitalized at what could have only seemed like a miracle to him—receiving his son back from the dead as it were. And I equally love that what helped Jacob turn the corner from unbelief to belief was the appearance of those Egyptian wagons. "Perhaps the grain, animals, and gifts could have been bought with the silver [the brothers] had in hand or had stolen, but not the wagons."[7]

Just like Jacob's faith wasn't blind, neither is ours. God through Christ has shown us Himself, and He's shown us His love through Jesus' death on the cross. I can't help but think of Romans 5:8, "But God *proves* his own love for us in that while we were still sinners, Christ died for us" (*emphasis mine*).

God cares deeply about our individual lives, and at the same time, He wants to use us in His far bigger story of redemption.

CONTINUE BY READING GENESIS 46:1-7.

Jacob had seen enough to convince him that Joseph was still alive, and so he set out with all his family for Egypt.

What was the name of the first place Jacob stopped? What did Jacob do there?

Beer-sheba is a significant place in the overall story of Genesis. Let's look at some other important events that happened there.

What took place in Beer-sheba according to the following verses? Put a short description next to each passage:

Genesis 21:33 (Abraham's experience)

Genesis 26:23-24 (Isaac's experience)

Both Abraham and Isaac experienced important moments with God in Beer-sheba. Now it was Jacob's turn to call upon the God of his fathers in the same place they had.

After Jacob offered sacrifices to the Lord, the Lord spoke to him that night in a vision. What did God tell Jacob not to be afraid of (Gen. 46:3-4)?

Look back at Genesis 26:2-3. How were God's instructions to Isaac different than what he told Jacob in Genesis 46?

God is able to work out His divine purposes in your life, not only in spite of the pain others have caused you but also because of that pain.

God had specifically told Jacob's father, Isaac, not to go Egypt, and He'd specifically led Jacob to the promised land of Canaan. Jacob might have been concerned about leaving Canaan for Egypt. He may have wondered if Joseph's and now all of his family's decent into Egypt ran counter to God's plan for his family and the generations to come. This move represented not only an enormous shift in location but also a shift in thinking. This doesn't mean God is fickle or unreliable, rather He was following His specific plan of redemption that was much larger than anyone could have possibly understood at the time.

According to Genesis 46:3, what did God say He would accomplish in Egypt?

TRUE/FALSE: *God promised great things for Jacob in Egypt, but Jacob and his family would have to go without God's presence since they were heading into a pagan land.*

Genesis 46:5 says, "Jacob left Beer-sheba. The sons of Israel took their father Jacob in the wagons Pharaoh had sent to carry him … " This imagery shows that Jacob was too weak to leave his home and lead his family to Egypt.[8] His sons would have to shoulder the responsibility to transport him there. Waltke points out, "The promises will not be realized through human strength but through divine grace. His sons now take charge in carrying out the migration."[9]

This was a great reminder for me. So often I weary myself, running here and there with my hair on fire, wheels spinning, toiling and striving to accomplish God's plan for Him, trying to make up for my failures, when—breaking news—I'm ultimately not capable and He's already accomplished it. Our human strength is not what's going to do the trick, only His divine grace will do.

RESPOND: How does this image of Jacob's sons putting their father in none other than the Egyptian Pharaoh's wagons show you that God has you and your life in His hands, fully able to accomplish His purposes in and through you?

Look again at verse 7. Who came with Jacob to Egypt?

We're given an important note in verses 5 and 7. This rescue wasn't for a chosen few. All of the brothers' dependents, their wives, and children came along too. We don't get their names, "[n]evertheless, they too—even those from a Canaanite wife and an Egyptian wife—are known by name and numbered among God's people."[10] Because Jacob's descendants are so important to God's overall story of redemption, the author of Genesis includes the specific names of the sons born to Leah and her maidservants and Rachel and her maidservants and even lists the son's sons (Jacob's grandchildren) by name.

FINISH TODAY'S STUDY BY READING GENESIS 46:8-27.

So far in our study we've been mostly looking at Joseph's story from a checkerboard perspective—lots of reactionary and sometimes unrelated moves that don't seem to be governed by a bigger plan. We're finally at a point where we're beginning to see God's much bigger plan of redemption playing out, a plan marked by patience and forethought. We're beginning to see that God, in and through all the little moves of His people in our story—some sacrificial, some selfish—is working out a great plan to turn the house of Jacob into the nation of Israel in the land of Egypt.[11]

God is writing a story of redemption that's all about one King whose name is Jesus—the King who will rescue His people from their sins.

SESSION SIX VIEWER GUIDE

THE PROCESS OF FORGIVENESS

Fill in the blanks as you're watching the Session 6 video. If you miss any blanks, your leader should be able to help and go over these with you.

1. Stay _tender_ and moveable.

2. Bless those you _think_ you have the _right_ to punish.

3. Forgive in heart and in _actions_.

4. Be a _ruler_ who _rescues_.

5. _embrace_ God's perspective.

NOTES

'God sent me to establish this.'

GROUP DISCUSSION

✛ What is something Kelly shared in the video teaching that really resonated with you? Why?

✛ Does forgiveness come easily or is it difficult for you? Explain.

✛ Share a time someone extended overwhelming forgiveness to you. Why was this important and significant in your life?

✛ What does it mean to forgive in heart and in deed? Explain.

✛ Discuss some practical ways you can seek to stay tender and moveable, as Kelly shares in the teaching video.

✛ Which of these words better describes you: condemning or rescuing? Explain. How can you be more gracious?

✛ How can you get God's perspective on a difficult relationship? Who are some godly mentors and adults God has placed in your life who you might seek for wisdom and advice regarding challenging relationships?

✛ Is there currently someone you need to forgive or seek forgiveness from? What's holding you back?

Session Seven

A REDEMPTION STORY

Writing my first cookbook, *A Place At The Table*, was unlike any process I'd ever experienced. First of all, you don't really write a cookbook as much as you cook one and then eat your way through it. When my dear friend, Regina Pinto, who also happens to be a renowned chef, and I decided to embark on this culinary adventure together we had no idea what we were in for. Besides the painstaking task of gathering and testing recipes, grouping them in meaningful fashion, and writing stories about them, we had to photograph all these creations.

More goes into cookbook photography than I could have possibly imagined. The first day of our shoot, Regina and I nervously pulled up to the building that was half test kitchen and half studio. Regina's responsibility was to swiftly prep and cook over 100 recipes in approximately nine days—I have no idea what she was so worried about. When they were ready, Teresa, our extraordinary food stylist, dressed each dish that was ready for the camera with finishing touches, such as chopped herbs, shaved chocolate, or perfectly piped icing depending on the recipe. A single stem bouquet here, a brass ladle there, a perfectly strewn napkin for good measure, and our photographer, Stephanie, was ready to snap the picture. If you're wondering what I did all those days, I was very busy "testing."

I'm indebted to this talented team because photography is essential to a cookbook. You have to visually portray what you're hoping your readers will cook. You can't just tell them; you have to show them.

I found myself gazing at certain creations and thinking, *So that's what berry panna cotta looks like, or I've never been confident preparing a charcuterie board, but now I can see it!* Pictures often tell us what words can't. Ironically, the opposite is also true: A cookbook full of beautiful pictures without any recipes would be a recipe for disaster. The success of your meal is dependent on a list of ingredients, exact measurements, and step-by-step directions. We need both image and instruction.

What I've always found particularly meaningful about the Bible is that it's both of these. In some instances the Bible gives us specific direction, while other portions are filled with exciting and compelling stories that show us more than they tell us. As we enter into our second to last week of *Finding God Faithful*, I encourage you to consider what you've observed about God and His attributes. Note what you've discovered about human behavior and how our choices to obey or disobey God affect our relationship with Him and each another. In many ways Joseph's story shows more than it instructs. But if writing a cookbook has taught me anything, it's that a good picture can tell us as much as a good recipe.

Day 1
AN UNTHINKABLE REUNION

Genesis 46:28-30

I wonder in what ways the Lord has done the impossible and the utterly amazing in your life. God is in the business of performing the impossible. Yes, for our future salvation through His death and resurrection, but also in the here and now—in the land of the living—through His life (Ps. 27:13; Rom. 5:10). We're going to get a picture of this in today's study. Praise Him. My soul needs it.

Today's reading opens the final scene of our story. We'll spend the next two weeks reflecting on the wealth of events that happen during these chapters but know we're transitioning into the final act of our story (sniff, sniff).

READ GENESIS 46:28-30.

RESPOND: What grips you the most about Joseph and Jacob's reunion and why? Explain.

God is in the business of performing the impossible.

Who did Jacob send ahead of the family to notify Joseph of his arrival in Goshen? (Circle your answer below.)

Judah   *Reuben*   *Asher*   *Benjamin*

Look back at Genesis 37:26-28. Why is this choice unexpected?

(Don't forget that Judah's place in this story continues to grow in significance. Hang on to these mentions of him as they'll culminate in a dramatic way in the final week of our study.)

More than twenty years ago, Judah split up father and son when he sold Joseph into slavery. Now we see him preparing the way for Joseph and Jacob's reunion. I have to believe the irony wasn't lost on Judah as he left his family and made the lonely trek to Egypt. Along that journey Judah surely recognized how God orchestrated all that happened, not to mention God's kindness to someone as undeserving as him—Judah's life was being spared during the worst of famines by the brother he'd sold into slavery. Certainly he would have recognized both the sovereignty and mercy of God.

What did Joseph do when he heard his father Jacob was in the land of Goshen (v. 29)? What kind of picture does this paint about Joseph's expectation?

Joseph hitched the horses to his chariot and went up to Goshen to meet his father Israel. Joseph presented himself to him, threw his arms around him, and wept for a long time.

GENESIS 46:29

RESPOND: What does Jacob and Joseph's reunion tell you about God's faithfulness, even when we've given up hope?

Describing their reunion, the CSB translation says, "Joseph presented himself to him, threw his arms around him, and wept for a long time" (Gen. 46:29b). Your version may say Joseph "appeared" to Jacob. This moment of reconciliation wasn't a result of happenstance or even an occasion God merely allowed to happen—He was in this.

After Joseph and Jacob's emotional reunion, Jacob said, "I'm ready to die now because I have seen your face and you are still alive!" (Gen. 46:30). This isn't the first time in Jacob's life when seeing someone's face was a divine experience. Earlier in his life, Jacob cheated his older brother, Esau, out of his birthright and deceived their father into giving Jacob the family blessing, even though it was supposed to go to the oldest son, Esau. Animosity boiled over to the point where Jacob fled his homeland because Esau vowed to murder him. Many years later the two brothers were set to meet again.

READ GENESIS 33:1-10.

How did Jacob describe seeing his brother, Esau, after being terrified to see him (v. 10)?

Though Jacob experienced remarkable encounters with God, the truth is, we have greater access to "God's face" than any of the people we've been studying in Genesis. I love reading about these exceptional moments in history because they remind me that any glimpses of God in the Old Testament are meant to point us to what we have in our glorious and divine Savior, Jesus Christ.

READ 2 CORINTHIANS 4:4-6.

How is the light of the knowledge of God's glory displayed to us?

READ COLOSSIANS 1:15,19-20,27.

How has God shown Himself to us? As a daughter of Christ, who dwells within you?

In Jacob's day, the divine and dramatic experiences of God's presence kept God's people going for years at a time, sometimes decades. They didn't have the indwelling of the Holy Spirit, the fellowship of the body of Christ, or access to God through the person of Jesus the way we do now (Heb. 4:16; 10:19-22). Every now and again someone would have an extraordinary experience with God that would redirect the steps of God's people or turn them back to Himself. Today, we have all the fullness of Christ in us through the presence of the Holy Spirit, not to mention the blessing we have in His Word and His church. Let's lean into these realities for the remarkable blessings they are.

I don't know exactly how Jacob's reunion with Joseph happened, but I picture Jacob scanning the Egyptian horizon, waiting to be reunited with his son. The son he once thought was dead was alive and standing in front of him.

This was a divine moment to be sure. Jacob knew that God had been in the business of appearing to His people, as we already noted today. Jacob had even encountered God's appearing to him at Luz and at Beer-sheba. But all of these divine appearances were pointing to the ultimate appearing of God through the person of Christ.

As Jacob stood on the foreign soil of Egypt, wrapped up in the arms of his son Joseph, I imagine nothing could have been more of a blessing to him than his son's appearing. Given the divine significance of the word *appear*, I can't help but think of a future reunion that is still to come: The appearing of Jesus as triumphant King. He won't be robed in Egyptian regalia but in the glory of God. He will wrap us in His arms, but instead of weeping, He will wipe every tear from our eyes. "Death will be no more; grief, crying, and pain will be no more, because the previous things have passed away" (Rev. 21:4b).

Day 2

EXALTED TO SERVE

Genesis 46:31–47:12

We've heard quite a bit about the land of Goshen over the past few days of our study. Historians aren't exactly sure what part of Egypt Goshen was located in, but it was likely in the Northeast part of the Nile delta.[1] The area was well watered and the pastureland abundant for raising cattle.[2]

BEGIN TODAY BY READING GENESIS 46:31–47:6.

How did Pharaoh describe the land of Goshen in Genesis 47:6?

The very one the family resisted was the one who would save them, settle them in the best land, and provide for them and their families.

TRUE/FALSE: *The Egyptians had a special fondness for shepherds in their culture.*

How did the Egyptians' view of shepherds end up benefiting Jacob's family?

Pharaoh went above and beyond Joseph's request to settle his family in Goshen by offering to put them in charge of his livestock. Joseph's faithful and loyal track record with Pharaoh paved the way for his family's favored status.

RESPOND: How does the way you walk out your relationships in faithfulness, integrity, and kindness benefit those coming behind you?

Judah was the one who went ahead of the family to help reunite Joseph with their father, but Joseph had the plan for how they were going to survive in Egypt. By instructing his brothers to tell Pharaoh they were shepherds, Joseph helped them secure a spot in the pasturelands of Goshen. Because the Egyptians detested shepherds, Pharaoh put them in an area all by themselves. (This is like when I bring Mexican food onto an airplane and nobody wants to sit next to me. Winning!) Judah and Joseph both played roles in preserving and leading the family, and each of their roles would continue to grow in significance.

CONTINUE READING, IN GENESIS 47:7-12.

How old was Jacob when he met Pharaoh? In what way did Jacob describe the years of his life?

Strikingly, God was about to give Jacob some more years and turn some of that hardship into lavish blessing. This picture of God's favor offers profound hope for any of us who, at a low point, might have characterized our lives in much the same way. God was in the process of redeeming those difficult years.

When Joseph presented his father Jacob to Pharaoh, who blessed whom? (Circle the correct answer below.)

Pharaoh blessed Jacob   *Joseph blessed Pharaoh*

Jacob blessed Pharaoh   *Pharaoh blessed Joseph*

RESPOND: Briefly look back at Genesis 12:3. How did this portion of God's covenant with Abraham influence Jacob blessing Pharaoh?

PERSONAL REFLECTION

Think of someone in your spiritual or biological family who is hard for you to love. How can you show love to that person? Be specific.

Here we find a fresh reminder that we're to bless those who don't share our faith, and certainly when they've been a help to us. Colossians 4:5-6 says, "Act wisely toward outsiders, making the most of the time. Let your speech always be gracious, seasoned with salt, so that you may know how you should answer each person."

Verses 11-12 are unexpected, undeserved, and altogether wonderful. They're the destination Joseph's dreams have been pointing to all these years—dreams over which the brothers were furious, dreams for which they hated Joseph. "'Are you really going to reign over us?' his brothers asked him. 'Are you really going to rule us?'" (Gen. 37:8a). Even Jacob rebuked Joseph over his dream. Part of their jealousy and anger was a result of their failure to understand the purpose of a ruler in God's kingdom. Throughout the Old Testament, God's leaders were to accomplish God's purposes for the sake of His people. I can't imagine Joseph understood all this when he first dreamed those dreams, but now we all finally see it: Joseph's rise to power wasn't for his own pride or prosperity, rather it was for his and his family's salvation and redemption, not to mention that of future generations. The very one the family resisted was the one who would save them, settle them in the best land, and provide for them and their families.

TURN TO MATTHEW 20:20-28.

How were Jesus' followers to look exceedingly different from the Gentile rulers? How does Jesus define greatness here?

It would have been Jesus' absolute right to call His followers to be servants while He reigned on an earthly throne. But Jesus calls us to be the very thing He was—a servant. He didn't use His authority to crush people or get ahead. He didn't look for people to serve Him, rather He looked for ways He could serve people. And, still, the most overwhelming piece of it all is that He died a shameful death on a cross so He could give His life as a ransom for us.

Jesus calls us to be the very thing He was—a servant.

RESPOND: Each of us has a sphere of authority, whether in our homes, schools, or extracurricular activities. How are you using your place of authority to serve others? Be specific about the ways you can use your influence and resources to benefit the people around you.

Returning to our place in Genesis 47, we can't close today's study without reflecting on the irony of Joseph's position as second-in-command of Egypt. Earlier in their lives, Joseph's brothers despised the thought of him becoming their ruler. Many years later, it was the best news they could have ever hoped for.

At first, the brothers resisted Joseph because they didn't understand he would be a ruler who rescues. We tend to think of rulers who oppress, step on the little people, or are simply out for their own good. But Jesus, far superior to our beloved Joseph, is a rescuing Ruler. He came to rescue us from enslavement to sin, and He has prepared a place for us to dwell in His presence when we pass from this life. But sometimes we forget that He came to give us abundant life on this earth, too! Are you resisting God's rule in your life? I've resisted Him at times. Sometimes I've thought His reign in my life would be crushing, not life-giving. But God's rule is always for our good because His ways are trustworthy, loving, and righteous.

RESPOND: If you're resisting God in an area of your life, surrender to Him today. Tell Him you want to walk in obedience to Him. He wants to settle you in the best land. In New Testament terms, that's the place of abiding in His presence and the goodness of His will.

Day 3
JOSEPH AND THE EGYPTIANS

Genesis 47:13-26

As I've mentioned before, every time we open the Bible we're making a cross-cultural journey, and it's not always to the same place. Sometimes we travel to the bustling city of first-century Corinth, other times to Nehemiah's 450 BC Jerusalem, or, like today, the land of ancient Egypt. Assuming we could actually visit those locations in their day, the unfamiliar geography and customs alone would be culturally confusing enough. How much more so when removed from these cultures by thousands of years? I'm sure you can tell by my very diplomatic introduction that we're in for a challenging read today. That said, I feel confident our minds will be stretched and hopefully our hearts will be enlarged after studying today's text.

PERSONAL RESPONSE

Who do you know who's not yet a follower of Jesus Christ? How can you specifically bless him or her?

READ GENESIS 47:13-26.

Besides the land of Egypt, what other land was experiencing severe famine? (It's mentioned three times in vv. 13-15. Remember the author of Genesis deliberately repeats what's important.)

RESPOND: Why do you think the author makes this deliberate mention of the other famine-stricken land?

To better see the progression of the famine and what was required of the Egyptians for survival, fill in the blanks below with the appropriate answers from the following word bank. (Some of your Bible translations may differ slightly from this language, but the answers should be clear.)

Land   Silver   Livestock   Themselves

Joseph collected _____ in exchange for grain.

Joseph collected _____ in exchange for food.

The Egyptians offered _____ and their _____ in exchange for seed.

TRUE/FALSE: *Pharaoh was the one who profited off the Egyptians, not Joseph. (See vv. 14,20.)*

RESPOND: Based on verses 23-25, how would you describe the Egyptians' response to Joseph's arrangement? In other words, did they feel good or bad about it?

The storehouses of God in Jesus Christ are abundant and accessible. Come to Him, for He has come to you.

I don't think there's any way around the fact that Joseph set up a system in Egypt that included a form of slavery to Pharaoh. Grappling with this as modern-day Americans, and more importantly as Christians, it's helpful to keep a few things in mind. First, the Egyptians were grateful for Joseph's offer, telling him that he'd saved their lives and expressing they'd found favor with him (Gen. 47:25). This practice is shockingly different from the American mindset, to be sure, where freedom is our country's middle name.

We also see that the Egyptians proposed the idea of selling themselves and their land to Joseph (v. 19); Joseph didn't suggest the idea. And since the Egyptians' livestock would have all died in the famine, you could argue that Joseph's purchase of cattle for food gave them something useful for what wouldn't have served them anyhow. The same thing goes for Joseph purchasing their land, which at that time could bring them nothing of sustenance.

All of these realities don't erase the troubling system of the Egyptians being enslaved to Pharaoh and the fact that Joseph dished it out. But they do serve as helpful windows into how the starving Egyptians viewed Joseph's plan and into Joseph's heart as an overseer. He was a steward, not a tyrant, a sustainer of life, not a profiteer.

LOOK BACK AT GENESIS 41:33-36.

I believe God had many purposes for raising up Joseph during the seven years of harvest and seven years of famine. What reason is specifically stated in verse 36?

RESPOND: As you consider the plight of the Egyptians in a desperate famine and God's goodness toward them through Joseph, what does this reveal about God's heart for the "outsider"?

When the Egyptians came to Joseph in Genesis 47:25, they said,

"You have _____ our lives."

I am moved by the storehouses of grain God saved for a nation that didn't worship Him or follow His ways. God raising up Joseph to bring grain both to Canaan and Egypt gives us a glimpse of what was to come on a much grander scale in John's Gospel.

READ JOHN 6:22-35.

Why were the crowds looking for Jesus (v. 26)?

TRUE/FALSE: *Jesus spoke of two types of food: food that perishes and food that lasts for eternal life (v. 27).*

Who gives the food that lasts for eternal life (v. 27)?

How does Jesus describe Himself in verse 35?

God used Joseph to save the Egyptians' lives. Surely the surrounding nations would have known about such a great salvation. As I think of Joseph and his grain that saved the Egyptians I can't help but think of the Bread of life who would one day give His very body and blood for all the nations of the world. "For the bread of God is the one who comes down from heaven and gives life to the world" (John 6:33).

Sometimes we consider the eternal bread found in Jesus as something less than the physical forms of bread we often set our hearts and affections on. If you're hungry, hopeless, powerless, or in the middle of a famine, the storehouses of God in Jesus Christ are abundant and accessible. Come to Him, for He has come to you.

Day 4

JACOB'S
FAITH REQUEST

Genesis 47:27-31

Today we turn our attention back to an important moment in Jacob's life. In his youth Jacob was a bit of a crafty, sometimes deceiving, sort of character. In the years after losing Joseph he appeared tired and a little forlorn.

After many years of fleeing from the storm he'd brewed in his family, scheming with his uncle for more money and cattle, wrestling with God, and losing his beloved son, regardless of how worn-out Jacob might be, God was still keeping His promise to him—Jacob would be blessed and made into a great nation. God's covenant wasn't dependent on how much faith or the lack of faith Jacob had on a given day—which somewhat ironically leads us into the next meaningful portion of today's reading. Jacob will finally exhibit some serious faith. The shiny, bedazzling treasures of Egypt that would have likely trapped Jacob earlier in his life were of no use to him now. God, His people, and His promises were all that Jacob was living for—and it had only taken him approximately 147 years to get here.

READ GENESIS 47:27-31.

By what name does the author refer to Jacob in verse 27?

We've alluded to Jacob's two names before, but today we're going to briefly look at how and when he went from Jacob to Israel.

READ GENESIS 32:24-32.

Who renamed Jacob and what explanation is given for why he was renamed Israel?

This section of Genesis is important to our study because it foreshadows who Jacob's family will become. In Genesis 47:27, when the narrator specifically says that Israel settled in Goshen, he's speaking about both Jacob as an individual and his descendants who would blossom into the nation of Israel.

How did Jacob's family fare in the land of Egypt?
(Circle the best answer below.)

   a. They acquired property.

   b. They became fruitful.

   c. They became numerous.

   d. All of the above

You may have noticed from our reading today we've suddenly moved to the end of Jacob's life, skipping approximately seventeen years. The Egyptians have been saved from the famine, and Jacob's entire family has more than survived it—they've thrived in it. Ironically, they've multiplied in Egypt while the Egyptians became slaves to Pharaoh in their own land. While the blessing and provision that Jacob's family experienced in Egypt was astounding, we can't forget how jarring this move from Canaan to Egypt must have been for the family—foreign gods, religion, customs, and landscape. But it seems those issues might have been the least of Jacob's worries.

LOOK BACK AT GENESIS 17:1-8.

How did the current location of Jacob and his family seem to be at odds with God's covenant with Abraham (v. 8)?

God's covenant wasn't dependent on how much faith or the lack of faith Jacob had on a given day.

Imagine the complexity of Jacob's situation. God had clearly led Jacob and his family to Egypt. He was blessing and providing for them within that land, but Egypt wasn't the place He'd promised to Abraham's (and by extension Jacob's) family. Jacob surely wondered if they would ever get back to Canaan. If they were to get back, how in the world would this happen?

LET'S RETURN TO GENESIS 47:27-31.

How many years did Jacob live in Egypt?

RESPOND: This is the same amount of years that Jacob shared with Joseph earlier in his life. What does this unexpected and significant number of years tell you about the good and ordered hand of God in both their lives?

As Jacob neared the end of his life, what did he request Joseph do and not do for him? List all the reasons you can think of that Jacob brought his request to Joseph instead of any of the other brothers.

RESPOND: Why do you think the place where Jacob was buried was so important to him? (Remember what you read today in Gen. 17:1-8.)

The longer I follow Jesus, the more the fleeting pleasures of this earth really do dim in comparison to the joy of His fellowship and the privilege of loving and serving people, pleasures that are eternal. The end of Jacob's life inspires me to live fully in view of God's promises, even the ones that might be a way off. Jacob could have made his permanent home in Egypt and identified with its prosperity, but he knew that none of those flash-in-the-pan riches could hold a candle to taking his place as part of God's royal lineage. Jacob would return to Canaan, even if just his bones made the trip.

TURN TO HEBREWS 11, AND READ VERSES 8-10,13-14.

Abraham, Isaac, and Jacob saw God's promises _____.

At night	*Close up*
From a distance	*In a dream*

RESPOND: Abraham, Isaac, and Jacob all lived in temporary and moveable tents. What does this tell you about how they viewed their life on earth?

What were they ultimately looking for (vv. 10,14)?

RESPOND: In light of these verses in Hebrews, describe how the faith of the patriarchs might look today. In other words, what would it look like to live with that same faith in our modern times?

Jacob finally knew what mattered. Even though he could only see the promises from afar, Jacob joined God in His promise, determined to return to Canaan even if it was for his burials. The promised land was not ultimately about the physical land of Canaan, rather it was pointing to an eternal city whose builder and maker is God. The ways of God we so often resist, once again, prove to be the paths of life.

Day 5
THE DOUBLE PORTION
Genesis 48:1-12a

I wonder if sometime during this study you've let yourself start hoping again. If you're like me, when God kindles a vision in your soul you eagerly fan the oxygen of God's Word and faith-filled prayers onto its growing flame. Sometimes the flame grows into a crackling fire beyond your imagination, and other times the flame is extinguished by betrayal, loss, illness, or just plain life. When disappointment happens, our hopes can evaporate as surely as embers give way to thin swirls of smoke. We snuff out the dream from our memories and go on our way. As the dream goes, so goes some of our hope and faith.

What we forget, or simply don't realize, is that sometimes dreams have to die for God to resurrect them. Even if a flame goes out, it's no match for a God who can relight it—and, yes, I do love a pun. As we continue to see God fanning His covenant promise to the patriarchs (Abraham, Isaac, and Jacob) into flame, be encouraged by the renewed hope God gave individually to Jacob and Joseph in our study. Yes, God was keeping His promise to Abraham, future Israel, and future nations, but don't miss for a second that while doing so He also lifted the hopeless head of Jacob, reviving his soul! He redeemed Joseph's story and would double his blessing. Dear friend, if the promise God has given you is in accordance with His Word and will, you keep hanging on. He's not out of matches.

READ GENESIS 48:1-12.

When Joseph set out to visit his father after hearing Jacob was close to death, who did Joseph bring with him? What surprising turn of events happened in verse 5?

PERSONAL REFLECTION

What's one temporary pursuit that's taking up a lot of your time and attention? How can you use some of that time for something that will matter for eternity? (It could be investing in a relationship, serving a classmate, or starting a prayer group, just to name a few.)

When Joseph's Egyptian wife gave birth to his sons in the land of Egypt, I can't imagine Joseph ever dreamed a moment like this was possible—that he would see his father again, that his sons would meet their grandfather, and most improbable, that Jacob would adopt Joseph's sons as though they were his own. This adoption didn't mean Jacob would raise them—he was at the very end of his life. It meant they would be full recipients of the divine inheritance granted to Jacob's family, as if Manasseh and Ephraim were Jacob's own firstborn and second-born, like Reuben and Simeon. Jacob would bestow his blessing on his two grandsons in exactly the same way he was about to bless his actual sons. Jacob had fifty-three grandsons, and Joseph's sons were the only two that were elevated to the level of sons (Gen. 46:7-27).

PERSONAL REFLECTION: When you think of the loss and hardship in Joseph's life, what does this unexpected blessing of his sons' elevated status tell you about God's redemptive heart?

Before Jacob explained his adoption of Manasseh and Ephraim, he recounted the time God appeared to him in Bethel (Luz) in the land of Canaan. In doing so, Jacob let Joseph know he had the authority to do what he was about to do. (Though God was with Joseph, there's no biblical record that He ever appeared to him the way He did to Abraham, Isaac, and Jacob.) This is kind of like when you were growing up and your mom told you to do something, and you asked, "Why?"

And then she gave you the universal reason, "Because I'm the mom."

Here, Jacob says, "Because God appeared to me."

Compare Genesis 35:11-12 with Genesis 48:3-4, and complete the exercises below:

TRUE/FALSE: *In both accounts, God is referred to as God Almighty.*

In chapter 35, God tells Jacob that part of his legacy will include _____, though Jacob's statement in chapter 48 does not mention it. (Circle the best answer below.)

> *Tribes   Land   Possessions   Kings*

When Jacob spoke of the land God promised to him and his future descendants, he was referring to the land of Canaan. Why did this now seem impossible?

No matter how seemingly impossible, Jacob was going all-in on the promise of God, the promise that one day his descendants would return to and inherit the land of Canaan. And by God's authority, Joseph's legacy wouldn't miss out on that inheritance even though Joseph was sold into slavery in Egypt by the evil actions of his brothers. His legacy, in fact, would double as Manasseh and Ephraim would be counted as Jacob's sons.

When Jacob, who was nearly blind, asked about the boys Joseph brought with him, he responded, "They are my sons God has given me here" (v. 9). Notice that simple word *here*—here, as in the land of Egypt. Joseph's confident proclamation that God had given him two sons in the land of Egypt, by an Egyptian wife, is profound. How beautiful and hopeful for all of us: no matter how distant the place we find ourselves in, how unorthodox or unexpected our situations are compared to what we think they should be, God's redemption is able to cross borders and restore what seems hopelessly lost.

God's redemption is able to cross borders and restore what seems hopelessly lost.

RESPOND: Look back at verse 11. Name one thing God has done for you that you never expected. Briefly write about it below.

This week we've overturned a few more pieces to the puzzle, and God's covenant promise has come into clearer focus. My earnest prayer is for God Himself—His mercy, redemption, power, blessing, and love—to have also become more radiant to you. Perhaps my favorite thing about all that we've studied this week is Jacob's recollection of God's words to him in Bethel, "I will make you fruitful and numerous" (Gen. 48:4). No doubt Jacob set out to accomplish the charge God had given him—to be fruitful and multiply. But all these years later, on his deathbed, Jacob realized that his life's vast fruit and multiplication had been brought to pass as a result of God's doing, not his own.

RESPOND: We close our week being reminded that we serve a God who always keeps His promises to us. What promise of God are you currently dismissing or disregarding? What change do you need to make in your life in order to live as though that promise is true?

SESSION SEVEN VIEWER GUIDE

A REDEMPTION STORY

Fill in the blanks as you're watching the Session 7 video. If you miss any blanks, your leader should be able to help and go over these with you.

1. Don't _forget_ what God wants to _redeem_.

2. God's redemption always _exceeds_ our expectations.

3. A _redemption story_ is only possible with a Redeemer.

NOTES

— REDEEM: TO BUY BACK —

GROUP DISCUSSION

✛ If you don't already know Jesus as your Lord and Savior or if you have doubts, leaders will be available during this time or after this session to talk with you.

✛ When have you given up on a promise from God? Describe the situation.

✛ When have you seen God redeem a situation you thought was unredeemable? Is there a part of your story that you still long for God to redeem?

✛ How has God's redemption exceeded your expectations?

✛ How has God been a Shepherd to you?

✛ Who in your sphere of influence needs to know the Redeemer? What are you currently doing to introduce him or her to God? Commit to praying for him or her each and every day this week.

A FAITHFUL FINISH

My dad has always been an avid walker. Between our neighborhood strolls together when I was younger and our hikes on vacation, taking walks has evolved into one of my favorite pastimes. I'm trying to pass on this healthy and relational activity to my seven-year-old nephew, Will, and six-year-old niece, Harper, in hopes of creating meaningful experiences with them like the ones I had with my dad. (My niece Lily is only two, so her time is coming.)

I may have been overly zealous in pursuit of this noble endeavor the day I talked Will and Harper into walking with me around a nearby lake. Its surrounding landscape is thickly wooded with mature trees, and it's home to deer, turtles, and an interesting variety of birds. It's one of our favorite places to visit. However, biting off the entire lake trail was apparently more than they bargained for. They complained about how their feet hurt, how their legs suddenly weren't working, and how huge this lake was, as though it had swelled into the Mediterranean Sea. "Aunt Kelly," Harper moaned, "Can we just turn around? I'm so tired!"

Turning around would have been a reasonable possibility except that we'd already crossed the halfway mark. Continuing forward was obviously the quickest route back, but try explaining that to a fatigued first grader. (I'm sincerely convinced that while Harper is at elementary school learning how to spell the word *elephant*, she's also preparing to take the Bar exam—she was kindly and respectfully arguing me into a pretzel.) The last half of our hike consisted of her relentlessly persuading me to turn around, and me trying to convince her that moving forward was the fastest way home. Oh the irony!

Harper's flawed perception of the best way forward wasn't lost on me. I'd let this faulty viewpoint like this mislead me in life on more than hikes. As followers of Christ it can sometimes feel that we're moving in the wrong direction, completely against what our internal compasses tell us. We determine that if we want to get home we best turn around. But if anything stands out to me about Joseph's life it's that while it seemingly started out in the wrong direction, toward Egypt, he never left the trail of God's purpose. And more importantly, God never left his side. As we close our study it is only fitting that by the grace and sovereignty of God, the circuitous route of Joseph's life would eventually lead him home.

THE UNEXPECTED BLESSING

Genesis 48:13-22

I wonder what life would have looked like for Jacob if as a teenager he could have somehow harnessed all the wisdom and clear perspective he had at the age of 147. But faith is typically forged through time, experience, and hardship. I suppose if faith came any easier it wouldn't be faith. In today's reading we'll find Jacob at the end of his life, rising up with humility, authority, and a God-given drivenness we haven't seen from him before. Jacob's faith budded in Bethel, grew in Haran, strengthened at the ford of Jabbok, faltered in Canaan at the loss of Joseph, and revived in Egypt. It would at last come into full bloom in his final days. By faith, Jacob would take hold of promises yet to come. I contend it will be his finest moment yet.

READ GENESIS 48:13-20.

Even though Jacob couldn't see Manasseh and Ephraim well, he was able to hold them in his arms. "I never expected to see your face again … , " Jacob said to Joseph, "but now God has even let me see your offspring" (v. 11). This right here is the lavishness of God. What Jacob couldn't have possibly imagined, seeing his son Joseph, God not only accomplished, but also exceeded by allowing Jacob to see his two grandsons.

In our efforts to avoid the prosperity gospel, sometimes I think we go too far in thinking our God is a God of scarcity instead of the God He really is, the God of abundance. The Old Testament teems with examples of God's spiritual and physical blessings upon His people, as does the New Testament. Paul said, "And God is able to make every grace overflow to you, so that in every way, always having everything you need, you may excel in every good work" (2 Cor. 9:8).

Jacob took an unexpected action when blessing his grandsons (vv. 13-14). Joseph wanted his father to put his right hand on his oldest son, _____.

Jacob insisted on putting his right hand on Joseph's youngest son, _____.

According to Genesis 48:17-18, how did Joseph feel about Jacob's choice of blessing the younger over the older? (In verse 13, we also see Joseph guiding his sons in the opposite direction.)

In ancient Israel, blessing the oldest son with a double inheritance was a custom. Joseph would have been attached to the idea of his firstborn, Manasseh, receiving the double portion from Jacob. When Jacob put his right hand on Ephraim instead of Manasseh, this signified a major shift in Joseph's vision and plan for his sons.

My mom and I recently texted about a situation our family wouldn't have looked for or ever thought to pray for. She said, "God's ways aren't always our ways; I'm open." Being open is especially challenging when it relates to our long and dearly held plans for ourselves and our loved ones. But this humble posture of openness to God avails us to what God wants to bring us and loosens our grip on how we think things should go. It also acknowledges our trust in God and His sovereignty.

Being open is especially challenging when it relates to our long and dearly held plans for ourselves and our loved ones.

TURN TO GENESIS 48:15-16.

While Jacob's right hand rested on Ephraim and his left on Manasseh, Jacob described God based on some significant experiences he'd had with Him. Fill in the blanks below (your translations may vary slightly).

> *The God before whom his fathers Abraham and Isaac had _____.*

> *The God who had been his _____ all his life.*

> *The _____ who redeemed him from all harm.*

WALKING WITH GOD

The Bible's description of the patriarchs having walked with God indicated their close relationship with Him, one that encompassed every facet of their lives. Jacob referenced Abraham and Isaac, and their intimate relationship with God, as a way of identifying himself with the God of his forefathers as well as attaching Joseph (and Ephraim and Manasseh) to Him.

> *According to Deuteronomy 30:15-16, what does walking with God look like?*

> *How does the prophet Micah describe walking with God in Micah 6:8?*

GOD AS SHEPHERD

Consider Psalm 23:1-4. What does God do for His people as shepherd?

How does Jesus fulfill the description of our Shepherd in John 10:11-18?

GOD AS PROTECTIVE ANGEL & REDEEMER

In Genesis 48:16, what did Jacob say the angel did for him?

What step of obedience can you take in the "here and now" that's based on what God has promised in the "yet to come"?

Jacob characterized God as his delivering angel. Your translations may vary using the word *redeemed* or *delivered*. This is rich with meaning, ultimately foreshadowing the coming of Jesus Christ not only as one who redeems but also as our Redeemer.

I don't think Jacob could have imagined that one day the God of his fathers would send His Son to be both Shepherd and Redeemer for the world. In much the same way, the blessing of salvation did not belong to us, but now it is ours through Jesus Christ.

RESPOND: If you have yet to surrender your life to Jesus Christ, our strong Shepherd and glorious Redeemer, pore over John 10:11-18 and Titus 2:11-14. Confess your inability to save yourself from the sin that has separated you from God, and receive the blessing of being made right with Him through the death and resurrection of Jesus Christ.

When Jacob blessed Manasseh and Ephraim as his own sons, he was actively taking part in God's promise for nations to come from him. Jacob trusted God would fulfill what Jacob would not see come to pass. In laying his hands on the heads of his grandsons, Jacob was laying hold of God's promises.

One of the most challenging and exciting parts of the Christian life is walking in obedience to Jesus now, while not always knowing when or how God will fulfill His promises to us in the future. This is precisely what makes faith, faith. And it ever pleases Him (Heb. 11:6).

Day 2

THE BLESSINGS OF THE TWELVE

Genesis 49:1-28

God's theme of blessing is central to the Book of Genesis. God blessed man and woman in the garden before sin entered the world, and He also blessed them after the fall. Despite sin wreaking havoc on relationships, destroying lives, and leaving the earth groaning under a curse, God's promise to Abraham—for land, descendants, and all the nations on earth to be blessed through him—has continued to press forward.

READ GENESIS 49:1-28.

We'll spend the bulk of our time studying Judah and Joseph's blessings, but we'll briefly look at the blessing of each son. Keep in mind these blessings focus on the tribes that will come from the sons as much as they are about the individual men. (The first six mentioned are Leah's sons.)

Then Jacob called his sons and said, "Gather around, and I will tell you what will happen to you in the days to come."

GENESIS 49:1

REUBEN

What did Jacob say would keep Reuben from excelling (v. 4)?

SIMEON AND LEVI

Simeon and Levi are paired together because of a violent incident they were both involved in. (You can read about it in Gen. 34.) What did Jacob especially take issue with in verse 6?

You might say the first three blessings are actually anti-blessings, and in a sense, they are. But considering Jacob's sons will ultimately form the twelve tribes of Israel, the fact that Reuben's sexual immorality and Simeon and Levi's unrestrained violence will not set the tone for the nation's leadership is a blessing for the nation as a whole.

JUDAH

Verse 10 in the NIV says, "The scepter will not depart from Judah, nor the ruler's staff from between his feet, until he to whom it belongs shall come and the obedience of the nations shall be his."

TRUE/FALSE: *The word* scepter *is a symbol of eminence and kingship. The kingdom ultimately belongs to someone who would come in the future.*

TRUE/FALSE: *One nation will be obedient to this ruler.*

Turn to Matthew 1 and read verses 2-6. What renowned king will come from the line of Judah (v. 6)?

    Moses   *Joshua*   *David*   *Samuel*

PERSONAL REFLECTION

What does the promise of Jesus Christ coming through the unexpected line of Judah reveal about the grace of God?

While Genesis 49:11-12 clearly points to King David's throne, we also see the promise of a messianic ruler who will sit on His throne for eternity. Jesus will be a mighty warrior who will conquer death and restore peace and blessing.

Let's continue with a very brief survey of the rest of Jacob's sons, leaving Joseph for last. (Note: Issachar and Zebulun are Leah's fifth and sixth sons. Gad and Asher are the sons of Zilpah, Leah's maidservant. Dan and Naphtali are the sons of Bilhah, Rachel's maidservant. Benjamin is Rachel's son. I'm so glad you're never going to forget this.)

ZEBULUN, ISSACHAR, DAN, GAD, ASHER, NAPHTALI, BENJAMIN

Generally speaking, how do the blessings of these seven sons differ from the blessings of the three sons before Judah (Reuben, Simeon, and Levi)?

JOSEPH

We'll spend the rest of today considering the blessing of Joseph. "He who was once separated from his brothers through spite is now separated from his brothers by blessing."[1] Only God could have accomplished this.

RE-READ VERSES 22-26.

How many times is a form of the word bless *used in Joseph's section?*

Throughout our study I've wondered how Joseph made it through the betrayal, loneliness, and separation from his family. How he was able to keep serving through the false accusations in prison and how he not only forgave his brothers but also lovingly sustained them through famine. The broad answer to these questions is found in the central underlying theme of our study: *God was with him.* By now I hope we are all clear that we can do nothing apart from God (John 15:5). But God's presence with us can sound so familiar and general that we stop hearing its meaning.

When "the archers" attacked him, what about Joseph remained steady and strong? How did this happen?

The only blessings that endure are the ones with which God Himself crowns us.

I'm struck by the obvious but deeply significant reality that God Almighty was the only one who could truly bless Joseph. Surely Joseph sought blessing from his father, Jacob, a blessing that came in the form of harmful favoritism and a multi-colored robe that attracted jealousy. Perhaps Joseph had wanted a blessing from Potiphar or Pharaoh, or maybe he'd always wished for it from his brothers. But in the end we see, the only blessings that endure are the ones with which God Himself crowns us.

RESPOND: Are you seeking blessing from a person, thing, or experience? No person or earthly experience will come close to satisfying your deepest longings. Spend time confessing this to God, and ask Him to help you seek the gift of His presence and the blessings only He can bring.

Verse 25 says the Almighty blessed Joseph with "blessings of the heavens above" and "blessings of the deep that lies below." I don't know for sure all the author meant by this metaphor, but the first thing I thought of was how many "blessings of the deep" Joseph had known—blessings in a foreign land, blessings in temptation, blessings in a prison. When Jesus meets us in the deep places, we never forget His presence or His blessings there.

God's grace is on full display here. God sent a Savior through those and to those who don't deserve it. And He raised up Joseph to save a nation, a foreshadowing of Jesus' ultimate salvation. I hope we won't soon forget Genesis 49:10. The One to whom the kingdom belongs has come. His name is Jesus. He will come again, and all nations will be obedient to Him.

Day 3
FUELED BY FAITH

Genesis 49:29-33; 50:1-14

Each person's character and choices matter, as we saw in yesterday's study when each son received an appropriate and fitting blessing. Somehow God put the actions of every person to work, both the good and bad, moving His plan of redemption forward. I will never grasp the mystery of it all, but what I know is this: I want to live a life fueled by a faith that sees past the grave, grasping the promises that live beyond it.

READ GENESIS 49:29-33.

Jacob instructed his sons to bury him in a cave in the field of Machpelah. In what important land was this burial place located? (Circle the best answer below.)

Canaan   *Goshen*   *Hebron*   *Bethel*

PERSONAL RESPONSE

How does Jacob's faith to identify with God's promises—even though they hadn't been fulfilled in his lifetime— encourage you to live fully in light of the eternal promises of Christ?

You may remember from our first week of study, Jacob was tricked into marrying Leah. Jacob went through the obligation of Leah's bridal week so he could marry Rachel, the one he truly loved. Now at the end of his life, Jacob could have told his sons to lay him next to Rachel near Bethlehem. He could have chosen to be buried in Egypt, the place he'd prospered with his family the past seventeen years, the place of his beloved son's reign. Instead, Jacob chose to be counted among his fathers in the place God had promised to each of them, an act of faith and quite remarkably an act of obedience. He finally understood that God's calling is deeper than our plans, our dreams, even our loves.

I thank God for the opportunities He's given me to choose Him and His ways over my personal desires, though it has never come easily. He has blessed my obedience with unexpected relationships, gifts, and opportunities. And where certain longings remain unmet, He is forging my faith and teaching me to live contentedly in the waiting.

CONTINUE BY READING GENESIS 50:1-14.

Describe Joseph's response to his father's death (v. 1).

Joseph worked hard on his relationships with both his brothers and his father. While we have no biblical record of Joseph resenting his father for the favoritism that set Joseph up to be hated by his brothers, I can imagine his emotions toward Jacob were complex and layered. In any case, Joseph put a lot of effort and care into his family relationships whether the family members deserved it or not. Joseph's emotion at Jacob's death displayed his deep affection.

> *What unexpected people group also mourned over Jacob's death (v. 3)? What other people group witnessed the mourning ceremony (v. 11)?*

And God heard their groaning; and God remembered his covenant with Abraham, with Isaac, and with Jacob.

EXODUS 2:24

By now you're well acquainted with the three elements of God's covenant with Abraham: God would give Abraham and his descendants land; his descendants would grow into a great nation; all nations of the earth would be blessed through him (Gen. 12:1-3). *All nations.* The groups who witnessed Jacob's burial were significant: his Hebrew descendants, the Egyptian officials, and the Canaanite inhabitants all took part. The nations were witnessing the mighty hand of God.

The elaborate picture of Jacob and his sons returning temporarily to the promised land accompanied by the Egyptian army foreshadows the further fulfillment of God's covenant with Abraham. Let's briefly look at what happened approximately four hundred years after Jacob's death, when a new Pharaoh was in power, a Pharaoh who knew nothing of Joseph and who despised the Israelites.

READ EXODUS 1:8-14.

> *One of Pharaoh's complaints about the Israelites was their enormous and increasing size. How is Israel's size significant to God's covenant with the nation of Israel?*

READ EXODUS 2:23-24.

> *What did God remember when he heard the Israelites' groaning?*

God raised up a leader named Moses to deliver the Israelites out of slavery in Egypt (Ex. 3). After substantial resistance, the Lord brought the Israelites through the Red Sea on their way to the promised land of Canaan.

What similar details are given in Genesis 50:9 and Exodus 14:23? Yet how are the circumstances significantly different?

The future nation of Israel would have noticed the irony of the high officials of Egypt, their horses and chariots, accompanying Jacob's sons back to Canaan to bury Jacob. This image "would have brought to mind the salvation of God at the Red Sea."[2] But for Joseph and his brothers, this was a long way off—an event they wouldn't see in their lifetimes.

How does Joseph's strong tie to his father inspire you to work hard at your most significant relationships?

RESPOND: What does Joseph's journey from Canaan back to Egypt tell you about God's timing? What does it tell you about living faithfully in the place God has you now while still clinging to His promises?

Today was a full day of study. You've done such a thorough job exploring the many layers of Joseph's story and tracing God's promises through it all. As we close today, two things are clear at Jacob's death: his desire to be counted among the people of God and his faith that God's promises would prevail, namely, that his descendants would inherit the land of promise.

Day 4
FORGIVENESS AND DIVINE PERSPECTIVE

Genesis 50:15-21

Joseph's complex relationship with his brothers runs like a thread from Genesis 37 to the end of the book. Just when you think that thread has disappeared into a family fabric of trust and serenity, the needle pokes back into their present. Though our trying relationships can get wearisome, there's something to be said for the sanctification that happens in us as a result of their trying nature. I've experienced some of the deepest heart transformation in the context of difficult relationships, especially when I've allowed them to mold me into the image of Christ.

That's the tidy way of putting it—I'm not saying it's always pretty.

On this second to last day of *Finding God Faithful* our story will return to Joseph and his brothers, the people with whom we started, and to the God who's been bringing about redemption all along.

READ GENESIS 50:15-21.

Joseph's brothers thought he might retaliate after their father's death. What does this reveal about their misunderstanding of Joseph's heart toward them?

PERSONAL RESPONSE

Why do you have trouble receiving forgiveness either from others or from God?

Why do you think the brothers had trouble receiving—or believing in—Joseph's kindness, love, and forgiveness toward them over the past seventeen years?

Why do you think Joseph wept when he learned about his brothers' fear of his revenge, thinking he hadn't forgiven them?

The CSB translates "Jacob's message" on behalf of his sons, "Say this to Joseph: Please forgive your brothers' transgression and their sin— the suffering they caused you" (v. 17). The Hebrew words used here for *transgression* and *sin* paint the strongest image of sin.[3] Joseph's brothers understood that their actions against Joseph were evil and horrifying; they also came to understand that these actions were sins against God. After acknowledging their sin to Joseph by way of sending the message, they threw themselves down before him in humility.

Perhaps you've thought that the only way you could forgive your offender was if he or she were to fall down before you, own his or her sin, and plead for mercy. But Joseph took no joy in his brothers' wallowing before him as slaves. Actually, this episode had no bearing on his forgiveness toward them. Joseph's emotional response toward his brothers showed he'd forgiven them long before that moment.

RESPOND: If Joseph's forgiveness wasn't based on what his brothers had or hadn't done, what was it based on?

RE-READ GENESIS 50:19.

Of all things he could have said, Joseph told his brothers not to be afraid. Have you ever been afraid as a result of your own sin? Maybe it was fear over the consequences? Fear over your sin being known? Fear over what your sin revealed about you as a person? In this moment, Joseph reflected the gracious and merciful heart of God toward sinners. If you've been afraid to draw near to God because of your sin, don't let fear stop you from coming to Him. As New Testament believers in Jesus Christ, His death and resurrection opens the way for us to draw near to Him "in full assurance of faith" (Heb. 10:19-22).

What place or role did Joseph not *assume (Gen. 50:19)?*

Joseph understood that he was not the Judge. He directed his brothers' attention away from himself and toward God, knowing the limits of his authority. One of the fundamental elements of forgiving others is realizing we're not in the place of God. When we forgive a person who's wronged us, we're placing the situation and outcome in God's hands. I can't help but think of 1 Peter 4:19, "So then, let those who suffer according to God's will entrust themselves to a faithful Creator while doing what is good." Joseph could forgive his brothers because he'd already entrusted himself to his faithful Creator, the One who knows hearts, the only One capable of judging righteously. And on top of that, he'd embraced God's perspective on his difficult circumstances.

In the space below, write out Genesis 50:20.

In many ways, Genesis 50:20 is the crux of the Joseph story. This passage by no means calls evil by another name, nor does it sweep harm and abuse under the rug of denial or head-in-the-sand oblivion. Joseph's statement is a head-on acknowledgment that evil exists in the world, and far more personally, that evil against Joseph existed. At the same time we find a parallel track of God's goodness and redemption, not running in place of evil, but somehow running alongside it, with God ultimately having His way with evil in the end.

RESPOND: Is there someone you've yet to forgive? Are you holding onto bitterness and anger? Put it before the Lord. Entrust yourself to Him. Trust that His plan of goodness for you hasn't failed. Forgive. Write your words of forgiveness in your journal or in the space below.

As you reflect on how God used Joseph's story for the redemption of many people, how do you see God using your unique life and story for the blessing of others?

According to verse 20, what ultimate purpose did God accomplish through His good plan for Joseph?

IT'S ONLY FITTING THAT WE CLOSE TODAY BY READING ROMANS 8:28.

What do both Genesis 50:20 and Romans 8:28 tell us about what God can do in any situation?

"You planned evil against me; God planned it for good..."
Genesis 50:20

I hope this study has helped you see the bigger picture of God's story of redemption through Joseph's story. In Genesis, God's plan for creation was good and His faithfulness to His people trustworthy. This remains true today.

RESPOND: How has a deeper understanding of God's plan of redemption through Joseph's story helped you more clearly see what He is doing today? How does this understanding affect you personally and the way you choose to live?

Day 5
FINALLY HOME
Genesis 50:22-26

Starting a Bible study of any kind requires courage and commitment. And coming to the end of one is best tied up with a ribbon of reflection. So my prayer is that you'll take the opportunity over the next few days to consider the truths you've learned from God's Word and the ways you can faithfully serve the Lord whether you're in the pit or the palace. I hope you'll never forget one of the things evidenced in Joseph's life: people who fail you can't prevent God's plan for you.

I'm so thankful for your perseverance in finishing this study. I will never be able to fully put into words what an honor it is to walk alongside you through my written and spoken words. It's one of the most fulfilling privileges of my life. I only wish I could hear your personal testimonies of how God is interacting with you based on Joseph's story and ultimately how you're *Finding God Faithful* through it all.

READ GENESIS 50:22-26.

Based on Genesis 37:2 and 50:22, approximately how many years did Joseph live in Egypt?

We don't know how old Joseph was when Jacob moved his family to Canaan from Paddan-aram, but we do know Joseph lived most of his years outside the land of promise.

LOOK AT GENESIS 39:2-3,21,23.

What recurring phrase is mentioned? How did this reality make all the difference for Joseph while living in a foreign land?

Throughout this study, I've been consistently reminded of a concept we began with: The God of promise is even better than the land of promise. That's not to say God's somehow disconnected from His promises. Rather, as we wait certain promises to be fulfilled, we experience His ultimate gift in His presence with us.

According to Joseph, what would God eventually do for his people (v. 24)?

PERSONAL
REFLECTION

What's the single most impacting truth or insight you've experienced in this study?

Hebrews 11 is often referred to as the Hall of Faith. In this chapter, the author mentions many well-known characters from the Old Testament and the specific ways they exhibited faith in their lifetimes. Joseph's mention in the Hall of Faith is succinct and somewhat surprising. Out of all the moments of faith Joseph could have been noted for, I initially found the author of Hebrews' choices interesting.

RESPOND: Why do you think the author of Hebrews chose to highlight these two acts of faith?

In Genesis 50:24 Joseph says, "I am about to die, but God ... " *But God* is one of the most powerful pairing of words we'll ever find in Scripture. Even though Joseph had been the savior of his family, the protagonist of a rags-to-riches story, and an impeccable picture of godliness, death was at his door. He'd taken his family—and the future nation of Israel—as far as he could take them. In reality, God was the One who'd carried the family, and God would be the One to continue the story that has been His all along.

Joseph told his fellow Israelites that God would eventually bring them out of Egypt and into Canaan "not because he had experienced it, but because God had promised it."[4] And that, I do believe, is the definition of faith.

Joseph made his people promise, when God came to their aid and moved them back to Canaan, to take his bones from Egypt and bury him in the land promised to Abraham, Isaac, and Jacob. Much like Jacob's action, Joseph chose to identify himself with the place of God over and above the place of his prosperity. By faith, he wanted to be counted among the people of God.

Hundreds of years later, after Moses, God would raise up a leader named Joshua to take the people of Israel into the promised land.

READ JOSHUA 21:43-45; 24:32.

What had never failed? What does Joshua 24:32 tell you about God's faithfulness to us?

READ JOSHUA 24:1-13.

These passages give us a helpful summary of Israel's story, beginning with Abraham up to the point of the Israelites coming into the land. It's encouraging to reflect on all that God did, even when it seemed at times that He'd lost control of the story.

As we bring our study to a close, I'd like you to look up Genesis 30:23, a verse you may remember from the beginning of our study. When Rachel held Joseph in her arms, what did she say that God had taken away from her?

Considering Joseph's story in light of God's covenant with Abraham helps us uncover a deeper meaning. When God made His covenant with Abraham, Abraham didn't know how the story would unfold. He only knew what had been promised, and he knew His God was able. When Rachel gave birth to Joseph, Abraham's grandson, and proclaimed that

PERSONAL
REFLECTION

Look back at Genesis 50:24 from today's text. In light of God's promise to bring Israel back to Canaan, do you think Joseph felt he was going in the wrong direction? Why or why not?

God had taken away her disgrace (reproach) through the precious gift of her son, little did she know that one day another Son would be given who would take away the sin of the world.

Even as we come to the end of Joseph's story we're not coming to the end of God's. As Joseph predicted, God eventually came to the aid of His people and delivered them from Egypt into the promised land of Canaan—those who came to Egypt as Jacob's fledgling family left as the nation of Israel. God prospered and patiently persevered with His people in Canaan even though they consistently wavered back and forth between obedience and rebellion. When Israel blatantly rejected God as their King and begged for a human king, God gave them what they asked for in King Saul and his disappointing reign. Eventually Samuel anointed God's chosen man for the job, King David. (As you know from our study, King David was a descendant of Judah, Jacob's son.)

Many generations came and went before the promised Messiah, the eternal King, was finally born in Bethlehem through the line of David. Indeed, Jesus was born a King but a totally different kind of king than Israel or the world had ever seen. He came to save His people from their sins (Matt. 1:21). He came to bear our shame on the cross (Heb. 12:2), and in so doing, He removed our disgrace and clothed us in His righteousness instead (2 Cor. 5:21). He conquered death through His resurrection. The blessing that came to Joseph through the God of Abraham, Isaac, and Jacob has now come to us in all its fullness through Jesus Christ.

I have loved studying the life of Joseph with you, and can't help but end where we began:

> You know, then, that those who have faith, these are Abraham's sons. Now the Scripture saw in advance that God would justify the Gentiles by faith and proclaimed the gospel ahead of time to Abraham, saying, All the nations will be blessed through you. Consequently those who have faith are blessed with Abraham, who had faith … Christ redeemed us from the curse of the law by becoming a curse for us, because it is written, Cursed is everyone who is hung on a tree. The purpose was that the blessing of Abraham would come to the Gentiles by Christ Jesus, so that we could receive the promised Spirit through faith.
>
> Galatians 3:7-9,13-14

God raised up Joseph to save a family, and He lifted up His Son to save the world. What a beautiful story it is, one no one could have written but God.

PERSONAL REFLECTION

What fear or attachment is still holding you back from taking a step of faith in your relationship with Jesus? Write a prayer of surrender to the Lord in your journal or the space below.

A FAITHFUL FINISH [Genesis 50: 15-18]

Fill in the blanks as you're watching the Session 8 video. If you miss any blanks, your leader should be able to help and go over these with you.

1. Don't _underestimate_ how many seemingly small choices make up a faithful finish.

2. No one on earth can _shatter_ a dream whose _source_ is in God.

3. A faithful finish has a lot to do with what side of the _semicolon_ you choose to live on.
   • [Genesis 50: 19-21].

4. A faithful finish is based on God's _promises_, not our present circumstances.
   • [Genesis 50: 24-26].

NOTES

• Don't mess up the small decisions; they all add up to a faithful finish.

• [Genesis 37:20] - Hatred from his brothers; the pit and his death.

• we can plan something evil, (whether we know it or not) but God can use it for good.

• Hebrews 11:22 (Joseph had faith; mentions THE exodus.)

• It's not the end of the story.

GROUP DISCUSSION

✛ What part of the video teaching really resonated with you? Why?

we can plan something for evil but God will use it for good.

✛ What does it mean to have a faithful finish?

To end life full of faith in God → strong faith

✛ How do the small choices we make contribute to our faithful finish?

small choices, like praying and thanking God just for life can strengthen our faith with Him, even if it's slowly.

✛ What has God put on your heart to do that you haven't acted on for some time?

✛ How have you seen God turn something meant for evil into something good?

✛ If you've suffered through brokenness, how can you live in light of God's sovereignty and goodness rather than wallowing in the wrong done to you?

By focusing on the future rather than the past. writing down my emotions.

✛ Would you say you are currently standing on the promises of God? Why or why not?

✛ Discuss some key themes you gained from this study and how you can practically apply them in your life in the days and weeks to come.

LEADER GUIDE

INTRODUCTION

Finding God Faithful is a video and discussion based Bible study for middle and high school aged girls. You will begin with the Session 1 video and then girls will read the Session 2 intro and complete the five days of personal study for Session 2 before your next group meeting.

LEADER TIPS

Be mindful of your girls and their family and life situations. The story of Joseph may bring to light and resurface suffering and trials that some girls in your group have faced or are currently experiencing. Be sensitive to this and mindful of their struggles and hardships. As much as possible, make sure you're available after each session to talk with girls who may have questions or need prayer.

PRAY DILIGENTLY.
Ask God to prepare you to lead this study. Pray individually and specifically for the girls in your group. Make this a priority in your personal walk and preparation.

PREPARE ADEQUATELY.
Don't just wing this. Take time to preview each session so you have a good grasp of the content. As you look over the group session and consider your girls, feel free to delete or reword the questions provided, and add other questions that fit your group better.

PROVIDE RESOURCES.
Each student will need a Bible study book. Try to have extras on hand for girls who join the group later in the study.

ENCOURAGE FREELY.
Cheer for your girls and encourage them to participate in every part of the study.

LEAD BY EXAMPLE.
Make sure you complete all the personal study. Be willing to share your story, what you're learning, and your questions as you discuss together.

BE AWARE.
If girls are hesitant to discuss their thoughts and questions in a larger group, consider dividing into smaller groups to provide a setting more conducive to conversation.

FOLLOW UP.

If a student mentions a prayer request or need, make sure to follow up. It may be a situation where you can get others in the group involved in helping out.

EVALUATE OFTEN.

After each session and throughout the study, assess what needs to be changed to more effectively lead the study.

NEW TO LEADING A BIBLE STUDY?

Prepare: Order a Leader Kit and Bible study books for the number of girls who are committed to be a part of the group. Become familiar with the Bible study content and preview the video session and review the Viewer Guide as you prepare to lead girls through this study. Make sure your meeting space is comfortable and conducive to conversation.

Watch: Prior to your meeting time, make sure the technology is set up and ready to show the video. The videos are 15-20 minutes in length, so prepare to set aside this much time of your meeting to watch the session video.

Review & Discuss: Use the Viewer Guide as a starting point to discuss what Kelly talked about in the video more in-depth with your girls. Set aside at least 30 minutes to spend in review and discussion of the video and then spend the last 10 or so minutes in prayer. Consider praying in pairs, but if you are short on time, simply close the group out as a whole.

Challenge & Encourage: Remind girls of the five days of personal study and encourage them to complete as much of it as possible. Be understanding of their schedules and that some weeks they might not get to all of the homework. Show them grace and continue to encourage them to press on each week as you meet, as well as at some point during the week so they stay mindful of the importance of studying God's Word and making their daily Bible study time a priority.

Connect: Stay engaged with the girls in your group through the use of social media, email, or text messaging. Make sure they know you are praying specifically for them. Seek to challenge and encourage them in their relationship with Jesus. Be available after each session to talk to girls who might want to meet one-on-one with you, or set up a time during the week to meet with these individuals who have questions or who desire to be further discipled.

LEADER GUIDE

SESSION 1

WELCOME

Welcome girls to the study and distribute their Bible study books if they don't already have them. Provide some time for the girls to introduce themselves, then pray for them and that God would use this study in their lives. Consider the following question if time allows.

 ✛ *In this study we're going to get a glimpse of Joseph's life story. If a biography were written about you, what would the title be?*

WATCH

Watch the Session 1 video, encouraging girls to fill in the blanks in their Viewer Guide on page 10 as they watch. Help them fill in any blanks they might have missed. The answers are as follows: 1. invitation; 2. set apart; 3. shoulders; 4. obedience.

GROUP DISCUSSION

After the video, lead girls through the Group Discussion section of the Viewer Guide on page 11. Feel free to adapt these questions so that they will work best for your group.

 ✛ *Challenge girls to consider one thing they want to gain from this study.*

CLOSING

Close your time together in prayer, as a group or in pairs, and challenge girls to work through as much of the Session 2 personal study days as they're able to in the coming week.

SESSION 2

WELCOME

Welcome girls to Session 2 of *Finding God Faithful.* Use the following questions to review their previous week's personal study.

 ✛ *How are you already seeing God orchestrating events in the life of Joseph? How does this give you confidence that He's working in your challenging circumstances?*

 ✛ *In what ways do you see the faithfulness of God in your life?*

WATCH

Watch the Session 2 video, encouraging girls to fill in the blanks in their Viewer Guide on page 30 as they watch. Help them fill in any blanks they might have missed. The answers are as follows: 1. depraved; 2. blessings; 3. spill onto; 4. land of promise.

GROUP DISCUSSION

After the video, lead girls through the Group Discussion section of the Viewer Guide on page 31. Feel free to adapt these questions so that they will work best for your group.

CLOSING

Close your time together in prayer, as a group or in pairs, and challenge girls to work through as much of the Session 3 personal study days as they're able to in the coming week.

SESSION 3

WELCOME
Welcome girls to Session 3 of *Finding God Faithful.* Use the following questions to review their previous week's personal study.

✛ *Why was Joseph especially vulnerable to temptation? When in your life do you tend to be most prone to temptation?*

✛ *Share about a time when you found God faithful after everything and everyone else had failed you.*

WATCH
Watch the Session 3 video, encouraging girls to fill in the blanks in their Viewer Guide on page 50 as they watch. Help them fill in any blanks they might have missed. The answers are as follows: 1. suffering; 2. kindness; suffering; 4. palace; prison; 5. fail us.

GROUP DISCUSSION
After the video, lead girls through the Group Discussion section of the Viewer Guide on page 51. Feel free to adapt these questions so that they will work best for your group.

CLOSING
Close your time together in prayer, as a group or in pairs, and challenge girls to work through as much of the Session 4 personal study days as they're able to in the coming week.

SESSION 4

WELCOME
Welcome girls to Session 4 of *Finding God Faithful.* Use the following questions to review their previous week's personal study.

✛ *Joseph served God in the prison and in the palace. Do you find it easier to serve God in times of abundance or times or great need? Explain.*

✛ *How can you be salt and light in your school, home, and neighborhood this week? Brainstorm some practical ideas as a group as you are reviewing.*

WATCH
Watch the Session 4 video, encouraging girls to fill in the blanks in their Viewer Guide on page 70 as they watch. Help them fill in any blanks they might have missed. The answers are as follows: 1. Holy Spirit; 2. eternal purposes; 3. storehouse; 4. don't forget.

GROUP DISCUSSION
After the video, lead girls through the Group Discussion section of the Viewer Guide on page 71. Feel free to adapt these questions so that they will work best for your group.

CLOSING
Close your time together in prayer, as a group or in pairs, and challenge girls to work through as much of the Session 5 personal study days as they're able to in the coming week.

LEADER GUIDE

SESSION 5

WELCOME
Welcome girls to Session 5 of *Finding God Faithful*. Use the following questions to review their previous week´s personal study.

+ *God was leading Joseph's brothers on a path of repentance. What did this week's study teach you about God's discipline and the gift of repentance (Rom. 2:4)?*

+ *So far, what have you learned from the ways Joseph has dealt with difficult family relationships? Explain.*

WATCH
Watch the Session 5 video, encouraging girls to fill in the blanks in their Viewer Guide on page 90 as they watch. Help them fill in any blanks they might have missed. The answers are as follows: 1. sin requires; 2. brother; ruler; 3. mercy of God.

GROUP DISCUSSION
After the video, lead girls through the Group Discussion section of the Viewer Guide on page 91. Feel free to adapt these questions so that they will work best for your group.

CLOSING
Close your time together in prayer, as a group or in pairs, and challenge girls to work through as much of the Session 6 personal study days as they´re able to in the coming week.

SESSION 6

WELCOME
Welcome girls to Session 6 of *Finding God Faithful*. Use the following questions to review their previous week´s personal study.

+ *What are some of the characteristics of a repentant heart? How did Judah display these characteristics?*

+ *How does Joseph's life and his actions point us toward the redemption Christ offers us?*

WATCH
Watch the Session 6 video, encouraging girls to fill in the blanks in their Viewer Guide on page 110 as they watch. Help them fill in any blanks they might have missed. The answers are as follows: 1. tender; 2. think; right; 3. deed; 4. ruler; rescues; 5. Embrace.

GROUP DISCUSSION
After the video, lead girls through the Group Discussion section of the Viewer Guide on page 111. Feel free to adapt these questions so that they will work best for your group.

CLOSING
Close your time together in prayer, as a group or in pairs, and challenge girls to work through as much of the Session 7 personal study days as they´re able to in the coming week.

SESSION 7

WELCOME

Welcome girls to Session 7 of *Finding God Faithful*. Use the following questions to review their previous week's personal study.

+ *Review the ways Joseph used his place of authority to influence those around him. How can you become more of a servant leader?*

+ *What earthly pursuit is currently taking up too much of your attention? How can you shift your focus to something of eternal value instead?*

WATCH

Watch the Session 7 video, encouraging girls to fill in the blanks in their Viewer Guide on page 130 as they watch. Help them fill in any blanks they might have missed. The answers are as follows: 1. forget; redeem; 2. exceeds; 3. redemption story.

Follow up the video with prayer, giving the girls an opportunity to receive Christ. Be available and also have other leaders available to pray and talk with girls about their decision to follow Christ. Follow up with them to make sure they are discipled and connect them with the student minister or girls minister at your church.

GROUP DISCUSSION

Then lead girls through the Group Discussion section of the Viewer Guide on page 131.

CLOSING

Close your time together in prayer, as a group or in pairs, and challenge girls to work through as much of the Session 8 personal study days as they're able to in the coming week.

SESSION 8

WELCOME

Welcome girls to Session 8 of *Finding God Faithful*. Use the following questions to review their previous week's personal study.

+ *How do you see the grace of God at work in the Messiah's being born through Judah's line?*

+ *What key truths are you taking away from this study? How will you apply these in your life and share the truth of God's Word with others?*

WATCH

Watch the Session 8 video, encouraging girls to fill in the blanks in their Viewer Guide on page 150 as they watch. Help them fill in any blanks they might have missed. The answers are as follows: 1. underestimate; 2. shatter; source; 3. semicolon; 4. promises.

GROUP DISCUSSION

After the video, lead girls through the Group Discussion section of the Viewer Guide on page 151.

CLOSING

As you conclude this study, remind girls of the key truths they're taking from this study. Challenge them to apply what they've learned in the coming days and months. Close in prayer.

NOTES

SOURCES

SESSION 2

1. James A. Swanson, *A Dictionary of Biblical Languages with Semantic Domains: Greek (NT)* (Oak Harbor: Logos Research Systems, 1997).

2. Jeannine K. Brown, *Scripture as Communication* (Grand Rapids, MI: Baker Academic, 2007), 226.

3. Kenneth A. Mathews, *The New American Commentary, Volume 1B—Genesis 11:27–50:26* (Nashville, TN: Broadman & Holman Publishers, 2005).

4. Ibid.

5. Ibid.

SESSION 3

1. Derek Kidner, *Tyndale Old Testament Commentaries, Volume 1, Genesis* (Downer's Grove, IL: InterVarsity Press), 204.

2. Ibid, 205.

3. "Definition of tsaraph," *Blue Letter Bible,* https://www.blueletterbible.org/lang/lexicon/lexicon.cfm?Strongs=H6884&t=CSB, accessed on March 24, 2019.

4. "Definition of Zaaph" BibleHub.com https://biblehub.com/hebrew/2196.htm, accessed on March 26, 2019.

5. Ibid, Mathews.

6. Ibid.

7. Ibid.

8. Definition of ruwts," *Blue Letter Bible* https://www.blueletterbible.org/lang/lexicon/lexicon.cfm?Strongs=H7323&tt=CSB, accessed on March 26, 2019.

9. "Lexicon for Genesis 41:16," *Bible Hub* https://biblehub.com/interlinear/genesis/41-16.htm, accessed on March 26, 2019.

10. John H. Sailhamer, *The Pentateuch as Narrative: A Biblical-Theological Commentary* (Grand Rapids, MI: Zondervan, 1992), 215.

11. Ibid, 215.

SESSION 4

1. Ibid, Mathews.

2. Ibid, Sailhamer, 218.

SESSION 5

1. John H. Walton, *The NIV Application Commentary: Genesis* (Grand Rapids, MI: Zondervan, 2011), 661, Retrieved from https://app.wordsearchbible.com on May 2, 2019.

2. Ibid, Walton.

3. Robert E. Longacre, *Joseph: A Story of Divine Providence, A Text Theoretical and Textualinguistic Analysis of Genesis 37 and 39–48* (Winona Lake, IN: Eisenbrauns, 2003), 47.

SESSION 6

1. Ibid, Sailhamer, 209.

2. John Newton, "Amazing Grace" 1779. https://library.timelesstruths.org/music/Amazing_Grace/, accessed on May 22, 2019.

3. Ibid, Sailhamer, 221.

4. Bruce K. Waltke with Cathi J. Fredricks, *Genesis: A Commentary* (Grand Rapids: MI, Zondervan, 2001), 566.

5. Ibid, Swanson.

6. Ibid, Mathews.

7. Waltke, 573.

8. Ibid, Waltke, 574.

9. Ibid, Waltke, 575.

10. Ibid, Waltke, 578.

11. Ibid, Sailhamer, 224-225.

SESSION 7

1. Brand, Chad, England, Archie & Draper, Charles, Eds. (2009). "Definition of Goshen" *Holman Illustrated Bible Dictionary*, Nashville, TN: B&H Publishing Group. Retrieved from https://app. wordsearchbible.com.] Accessed on April 26, 2019.

2. Benson Commentary, "Genesis 45:10" *Bible Hub*, https://biblehub.com/commentaries/genesis/45-10.htm, accessed on April 26, 2019.

SESSION 8

1. Victor Hamilton, *The New International Commentary: The Book of Genesis, Chapters 18-50* (Grand Rapids, MI: Eerdmans Publishing Company, 2010), 679. Retrieved from https://app. wordsearchbible.com, accessed on April 30, 2019.

2. Ibid, Mathews.

3. Ibid, Waltke, 622.

4. Craig R. Koester, *The Anchor Bible Commentary: Hebrews, A New Translation with Introduction and Commentary* (New York, NY: Doubleday, 2001), 500.

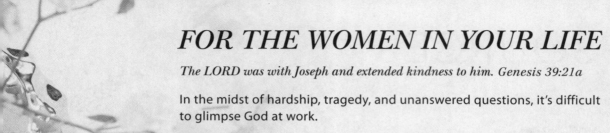